About the author

Rosaleen Moorhead-Murphy was born in Liverpool where she trained as a teacher. Writing and illustration have always been her main focus.

After their marriage, she and her husband, Pat, moved to Suffolk where their four children were born. Her first book, *The Mystery*, was published then and was an update of the medieval miracle plays where each scene could be prepared independently and presented as part of a whole.

The family then moved to the Scottish Borders where they had a painting studio and gallery, and it was there that she first visited Floors Castle, the seat of the Dukes of Roxburghe, and heard the story of the 8th duke and his feisty, millionaire bride, May Goelet. Further research resulted in *The Mayflower and the Thistle*.

The Mayflower and the Thistle

Also by Rosaleen Moorhead-Murphy

The Mystery (Geffory Chapman, 1969)

Ling Foo's Hat

A Duke's Diary – the diary kept by the 8th Duke when on duty with the future George V on the Commonwealth Tour 1901 to open the first Federal Parliament in Australia.

Rosaleen Moorhead-Murphy

The Mayflower and the Thistle

Vanguard Press

VANGUARD PAPERBACK

© Copyright 2018
Rosaleen Moorhead-Murphy

The right of Rosaleen Moorhead-Murphy to be identified as author of
this work has been asserted by her in accordance with the
Copyright, Designs and Patents Act 1988.

All Rights Reserved

No reproduction, copy or transmission of this publication
may be made without written permission.
No paragraph of this publication may be reproduced,
copied or transmitted save with the written permission of the publisher,
or in accordance with the provisions
of the Copyright Act 1956 (as amended).

Any person who commits any unauthorised act in relation to
this publication may be liable to criminal
prosecution and civil claims for damages.

A CIP catalogue record for this title is
available from the British Library.

ISBN 978 1 784653 88 0

*Vanguard Press is an imprint of
Pegasus Elliot MacKenzie Publishers Ltd.*
www.pegasuspublishers.com

First Published in 2018

**Vanguard Press
Sheraton House Castle Park
Cambridge England**

Printed & Bound in Great Britain

Dedication

Patrick Murphy, my husband, for support and photography. Gabrielle, my eldest daughter, for her excellent critiques; Nikki, Annette & Dominic, my other children & grandchildren; Sinead Crissi, Beth, Joseff (Welsh spelling) and Erin.

Acknowledgments

Sir Guy David Innes Kerr, 10th Duke of Roxburgh, for allowing me to enter this fascinating story by accessing so many wonderful documents and his encouragement.

Foreword from the Duke of Roxburghe, Grandson of Kelso and May

It is a great pleasure to have been asked to write the foreword to *The Mayflower and the Thistle*. It is the story of a beautiful young American lady from a very rich high society New York family who travels over to Europe accompanied by her mother who has keen ambitions for her daughter to find an aristocratic titled husband.

The book gives a fascinating insight into the world of high society either side of the Atlantic and how this strong willed, highly principled young girl sticks to her guns and refuses to accept the marriage proposals of a variety of British and European aristocratic suitors, and ultimately marries my grandfather, a handsome but shy Scottish landowner.

The result is a marriage full of love and happiness so unlike many between American heiresses and impoverished European noblemen of the time, and Rosaleen Moorhead-Murphy has written an illuminating account of life in America and Britain at the turn of the 19th century.

Roxburghe

Chapter 1
Marriage Matters

On the 6th October 1880, a daughter was born to one of New York's wealthiest couples, Mary and Ogden Goelet. She was named May, and, from the start, she was destined for a marriage of consequence.

Her pedigree was impeccable. Ogden was a banker and real estate magnate, who had inherited an already immense fortune in both property and wealth from his grandfather, Peter Goelet, which he had further enhanced, so earning for himself a respected place among the leading, multi-millionaire families of New York. His wife, Mary Wilson Goelet, was also socially well placed in her own right. She was one of the four children of TR Wilson, a man of great wealth and position, but, as her brother and three sisters had chosen to marry exceedingly well, she now belonged to a family network that included the most influential families in New York plus a British Duke.

Mary Wilson Goelet revelled in the privileges of such connections, which opened for her every desirable door in American society. Moreover, she was herself acclaimed as one of *the* most accomplished and much sought after hostesses, not only on the American scene but also in Europe. This delighted Mary, and she cherished the prominent niche she and Ogden carved for themselves in Paris, the Mediterranean and, most of all, in Britain.

They had just two children, Robert and May. Mrs Goelet was confident that, as their only son, Robert would one day step into his father's footsteps, and therefore could be guaranteed a successful future, so she was happy to let his life unfold without intervention. But, when May was born, Mrs Goelet saw the opportunity to achieve what had secretly become her dearest desire. She now dreamt of elevating her family into a full relationship with aristocracy one day through a carefully chosen marriage for this young girl. All around her she saw other mammas similarly launching their precious daughters so she resolved to wait, to plan – and - to make the necessary connections, which would one day, when May was old enough, stand her in good stead.

Hence, May's education was chosen to prepare her for such a future – an education that was, in fact, to be broader and more enlightened than that offered to many of her sisters in Europe.

To Ogden, it was simply May's preparation for the life as wife to an eligible, wealthy American, for he harboured no desire to see his beloved daughter married off in a deal to salvage some young nobleman's failing fortunes.

By the time May entered her teens, both parents were justifiably proud, as she was already showing the potential of becoming a beautiful young woman, both witty and intelligent. Her mother watched with quiet satisfaction, growing more and more sure that *her* secret ambition had every possibility of becoming a reality.

The old century was drawing to its close, and modern luxury, coupled with the comparative speed of the relatively new steamship travel, had brought an even greater influx of young, well-born bachelors to visit America.

The attraction of a society where one's social status was established by wealth brought a completely new dimension into the field of marriage prospects for aristocrats from the Old World. Hitherto, the search for a marriage partner was exclusively limited to alliances with families of equal bloodline, most of whom they had grown up among socially. Hence, young nobility married into other established noble families, either in Britain or within Europe. No greater example of this could be seen than in the British Royal family, as each surviving child of Queen Victoria's large family had married or would marry into one of the major Royal Houses of Europe.

But, with the economic upheaval of the Industrial Revolution, the clear definition between the classes was beginning to blur as a new, wealthy but non-aristocratic class emerged, especially in Britain. Although it was inconceivable for aristocrats to consider members of the nouveau riche in society as eligible marriage partners, nevertheless it was this very group which was increasingly in control of the wealth. At the same time, aristocratic fortunes were vanishing, as the upkeep of castles, mansions and vast estates became more and more financially crippling.

Moreover, new technology had opened up a variety of lucrative prospects for ordinary folk with a will to work, and, for the first time, opportunities appeared with the real promise of a new life away from traditional, agricultural work bound to great houses and from the varying forms of domestic service therein. For some, it was release; for many others the reality was that they were to trade one form of service for another, which often bordered on slavery, lacking the old securities of home and care that were usually intrinsically bound up in service on landed estates. This transition, nevertheless, meant that no longer were so many people dependent on lords and noblemen for their livelihood, and the possibility of independence became ever more attractive, so men and women left the countryside to gravitate towards the growing industrial towns.

Inevitably, the realization dawned on many young noblemen that not only were they facing chronic financial difficulties in maintaining their own family estates back home, but so also were the families of the young ladies whom they would hitherto have approached to find a bride - and a dowry.

Meanwhile, more convenient travel to America introduced these heirs of such estates and lofty titles to a totally new, and exciting class of young ladies, who could indeed be considered acceptable as potential brides. They were the daughters of the financial 'aristocrats' of the unprecedentedly wealthy New World. Their upbringing, although *modern*, had been as exclusive as that of the well-born young ladies back home, but their fortunes exceeded anything that was imaginable in Europe at that time, and so they seemed to offer financial salvation to many eligible bachelors in straightened circumstances.

On the other side, American matrons, like Mrs Goelet, yearned to have their daughters elevated to duchesses or even to princesses, so they welcomed and feted the sons of impoverished noble families who were, in turn, being pressurized by their families to undertake these contracts in order to rescue their ancestral estates. Consideration of the *feelings* of the young people involved were seldom considered to be relevant in such dealings by their elders, any more than they had been previously in Europe in the long-established custom of the arrangement of aristocratic marriages.

*****

It was at such a marriage that young May Goelet was to step onto Society's stage, for when May was fifteen she was invited by Mrs William K Vanderbilt to be a bridesmaid at the wedding of her daughter, Consuelo, and the Duke of Marlborough in 1895. For a young girl not yet *presented* in Society, it was a magical experience with all the apparent ingredients of a fairytale.

Little did she know then how radically that day was to influence and direct her life for the next nine years. Little did she guess that her mother was seeing this as a dress rehearsal for what *she* dreamed would be an even grander occasion that she determined to conduct one day in the future.

Yet it is true that May *was* to learn a lesson that day, which was forever to colour her attitude to marriage. For no other marriage was yet to be seen as quite so mercenary or heartless as the marriage between Consuelo Vanderbilt and Charles Spencer-Churchill, the 9th Duke of Marlborough.

The young duke had both inherited and incurred severe debts, for which there seemed to be no solution. Already he had been forced to sell his London mansion, Marlborough House, to the Prince of Wales to help support his failing country seat, Blenheim Castle. The fact that he was in love with someone else at the time was not considered of importance when weighed against his debts and responsibilities. Hence, he crossed the Atlantic in response to the very positive approaches he had experienced from the extremely forceful Mrs William K. Vanderbilt on behalf of her daughter, Consuelo.

The fact that these two young people had met while holidaying in the Mediterranean the previous summer and had shown absolutely no interest in each other was ignored. Even a visit to Marlborough's home, Blenheim Castle, before they returned home, had not captured Consuelo's imagination. Consuelo was as unimpressed by Marlborough's elevated position as Marlborough was by Consuelo's undoubted beauty and elegance, despite her millions.

However, when no other solution presented itself for his problems, a marriage contract became inevitable for him, hinging on the issue of her dowry, which was set at $10,000,000. This he discussed in New York with animated fervour, together with Mr Vanderbilt and the lawyers, after which he conducted a minimal and formal 'courtship' with a desolate Consuelo, which, in turn, led to an exceedingly cool proposal, lacking either passion or feeling.

Consuelo, herself, was also in love with someone else, and had promised herself to him in a secret engagement, so she was totally unmoved by her reluctant suitor. But her formidable mother had made *her* wishes clear. She scornfully and totally dismissed Consuelo's declaration of love for the man she considered to be her fiancé as nothing but an infatuation; a passing fancy; and reminded her daughter that she had no right to make any alliance without permission. Finally, she assured

Consuelo that she would actually shoot any young man who approached without her express consent.

There then followed a period during which she placed Consuelo under what can only be described as 'house arrest', and Consuelo could not leave the house unescorted; nor was she allowed to receive either guests or mail. Thus it was impossible for her even to get a message out to anybody, as there was, as yet, no phone, and every servant had been forbidden to handle any missive from her without it being censored by Mrs Vanderbilt herself.

Nevertheless, Consuelo tried to stand her ground and refused to marry Marlborough. Immediately, there was a crisis as her mother 'collapsed' and took to her bed, claiming to have had a heart attack. The hastily summoned doctor, a close family friend, seemed to endorse this diagnosis.

Then Mrs Jay, a friend and confidante of the intrepid Mrs Vanderbilt, hastened from the 'sick room' to visit Consuelo in her suite, where she subjected the poor girl to the worst form of emotional blackmail. She described vividly how ill Consuelo's mother, *her* dear friend, was, and that the only way to save her life was by Consuelo changing her mind and accepting the Duke's proposal.

Mrs Jay graphically described to the distraught girl that if she still refused the marriage, then she would thereafter have to live with the '*inevitable consequence'*. Although she never actually said the words directly, she definitely left Consuelo with the belief that, unless she should capitulate, her mother would die.

She was eighteen years old, broken-hearted, and still coming to terms with her parents' recent divorce, so Consuelo gave in and accepted the ungracious Marlborough.

With indecent haste, her mother miraculously enjoyed an instant and apparently full recovery, and left her room without delay to throw herself energetically into preparing the wedding that, she intended, would set all America - and indeed, all England - talking!

Incredibly, just days after her 'recovery', a wedding dress was delivered from Paris for Consuelo. So confident had she been of the success of her match-making, that Mrs Vanderbilt had chosen and ordered the dress, without consultation with her daughter, while holidaying in France during the previous summer season.

After its arrival, she saw fit to explain condescendingly that, as Consuelo was so young and her fashion tastes as yet immature, it had been necessary to make the choice on her behalf, so that it would be appropriate to her future position as the bride of a duke.

*****

It was from the day of May's invitation to be a bridesmaid for the Marlborough wedding that Mrs Mary Wilson Goelet's master plan for the future of her only daughter really began to take shape.

In her long-harboured dreams of future aristocratic advancement for fifteen-year-old May, she could not have envisaged so perfect a launch as the one now presented. It was the catalyst that was to fuel her maternal ambition, which was, in turn, to power her management of May's future.

In her mind's eye, she felt that May would step into her

own fantasy so influenced would she be as she walked up the aisle with the seven other bridesmaids as they led Consuelo towards her ducal crown - and it would be a dream, she believed, that would nurture in her the ambition to follow suit one day.

Mrs Goelet was very aware that the imminent marriage of her own younger sister, Grace, to Cornelius Vanderbilt Jnr was to mean that May was soon to be actually related to Consuelo; and therefore, by default, she would also be related to the Duke of Marlborough himself, and would be accepted in their circles as family.

To a daughter of T.R. Wilson, such relationships were very important to Mrs Goelet. As already mentioned, each of her siblings had seen it as their responsibility to marry well. Her brother, Orme, had married Caroline Astor, daughter of *the* Mrs Astor, also called Caroline, the arch-hostess of the New York set. For anyone to be considered acceptable in New York Society, it was deemed essential to be included on Mrs Astor's famous guest list, so to be actually *related* to the grand lady was considered the epitome of excellence.

This niche in the heart of Society had been further secured by her own marriage to Ogden Goelet, who, in addition to being a banker, was described as owning *vast areas* of New York: "*including the Imperial Hotel, the Knickerbocker Theatre, the building where Sherry's now stands, and that section of land extending from the Windsor Hotel to the East River.*"

The Goelets actually lived with Robert and May in a palatial mansion on Park Avenue, and, in 1888, Ogden had commissioned Richard Morris Hunt, America's foremost architect of the time, to design *Ochre Court*, which was to be the first of a group of houses in the *Grand Manner*, which was to develop Rhode Island into a millionaire's paradise of summer residences. It was a fabulous mansion, built of limestone high on the reddish cliffs, overlooking the Atlantic, and was inspired by the design of ancient French chateaux and churches, except in that it also seemed to reach over the cliffs like a great ship, affording breathtaking views of the ocean, for Ogden's great passion was sailing and he was rated as a world-class yachtsman.

But the Wilsons had long hankered after connections with British aristocracy and Mrs Goelet's other sister, Belle, was married to Michael Henry Herbert, or 'Minga', who was a younger brother of the Earl of Pembroke. And if Mrs Goelet would have preferred that he had been the older brother, it did not mar their friendship, nor did it prevent her from using the extended benefit of being directly connected to the Pembrokes when in Britain, which was always cordially reciprocated.

Hence the thought of having her own daughter actually married to a duke, or even better to a prince, was to shape Mrs Goelet's social programming until she achieved her ambition. And she was confidently aware of her ever-growing reputation as one of the leading hostesses in New York, Rhode Island, and, increasingly so, in London.

Nevertheless, despite all this opulence and social success, Mrs Mary Wilson Goelet was as dazzled as her friend Mrs Vanderbilt by the glamour of this glittering nuptial prize, which would, of its nature, bring with it the prospect of being closely connected to the court of Queen Victoria. Even though Ogden and herself had entertained Her Majesty in the Med on board their former yacht, the *White Ladye,* and when in England were regular guests of or hosts to the Prince and Princess of Wales, to actually have a claim of true relationship with the monarchy was the ultimate prize.

This promise, to her mind, would bring any young bride joy and fulfillment in itself, and would automatically overcome any perceived drawback in a relationship between virtual strangers. Nevertheless, even she must have been aware of the blatant monetary motivation for the Marlborough wedding, because the newspapers of the day exploited every twist and turn of the saga. The fact that William K and Mrs Vanderbilt had recently divorced seemed to unleash an unprecedented expose of intimate details that may have been withheld were it not for this fact; particularly as they portrayed Mrs WK as the heartless power force in the affair.

Impervious to criticism, the lady herself gave the press the ammunition for an open season when she made no secret of the fact that she would only allow the bride's father to attend the ceremony long enough to perform his duty in giving his daughter away, but would not be welcome at the reception. Gossip columns also buzzed with revelations that Consuelo had been instructed to return all Vanderbilt wedding presents, except those of her grandmother, who was the only Vanderbilt on the invitation list. Obviously, this poor lady was put in an impossible situation and eventually refused to attend because of the slight to the rest of her family.

But, in the pursuit of the *ideal marriage*, such prattle could comfortably be dismissed by the ambitious Mrs Wilson Goelet. She herself had made a highly successful marriage of her own *good match*, according to the standards of their day, and it was beyond her comprehension (as it was to Mrs WK Vanderbilt despite her recent divorce) that an arranged marriage into European aristocracy – if not royalty – should be the natural aspiration, one day, for her beautiful, raven-haired daughter, May. And as the only daughter and co-heir with her brother, Robert, Mrs Goelet's focus seemed sound and her prospects secure.

Hence, when May was invited to be a bridesmaid to Consuelo, her mother accepted with delight and saw it as her first step to, at the very least, a ducal coronet – or maybe even a crown. May was to be seen in public, before her presentation in Society, as a chosen companion of the future Duchess of Marlborough, to whom, very soon, she would also be closely allied through marriage.

This second connection with British aristocracy necessarily provided a far more assured initiation to eligibility than mere fortune, in her mother's eyes. And from that day, Mrs Wilson Goelet secretly planned that her daughter would actually marry a prince, and thus outrank even the Marlboroughs themselves.

May naturally had no idea of all that was going on behind the scenes with the Vanderbilts, nor of her own mother's burgeoning ambitions. To her, at fifteen, the thought of being part of this fairytale wedding ceremony was in itself a dream. She had known the older girl most of her life and had particularly spent time with her during holidays on Rhode Island and on their respective yachts in the Mediterranean, but the difference in their ages left May somewhat in awe of Consuelo. Therefore, she was flattered when invited to be a bridesmaid, totally unaware that Consuelo had had no say in the choice of her bridesmaids, but that she had been chosen by Mrs Vanderbilt because she fitted the required social profile.

Unawareness of these matters enabled May to revel in all the preparations; the fitting for the lovely white dress with the flowing sky-blue sash; the setting of her hair under the picture hat, which so complimented her striking brunette colouring; and the feeling of being adult at last when she attended the rehearsals and the pre-nuptial dinner.

If she noticed Consuelo's strained, distant manner and air of detachment, she would have assumed that it was either wedding nerves or just that she was overwhelmed with the enormity of what she had to remember for the ceremony in presence of all of America's grandest people – not to mention those accompanying the Duke.

It never crossed the young May's mind that this friend she had grown up alongside was being forced to embark on a marriage to which she was totally opposed.

Hence, the day dawned and a joyful May joined the other bridesmaids to be brushed and powdered by their maids in 660 Fifth Avenue and, crucially, it was at this point that, for her, fantasy met reality.

She learned, despite the taboo on gossiping with below-stairs staff, that Consuelo was a very reluctant bride. Moreover, to prevent her running away and escaping marriage altogether, she had been imprisoned in her room, at the express wish of her very own mother, to be released only for the rehearsal and for the pre-wedding dinner, until the moment she was to leave the house escorted by her father for the ceremony. To make sure that her instructions were obeyed, Mrs Vanderbilt had posted a footman on guard at Consuelo's door, with strict instructions that no-one but Consuelo's personal maid should be allowed to enter; not even her former governess who had become her closest friend.

Hence, when their hostess appeared to appraise their readiness to leave for the church she glowed with supreme satisfaction at the appearance of the eight refined young ladies, all exquisitely dressed in the gowns she herself had chosen to provide an excellent, if expensive, foil to the bridal outfit. However, they felt subdued.

Moreover, they were unprepared for the arrival of the bride as they crossed the hallway to step out into their carriages. She appeared at the top of the wide, flower-festooned staircase, and instead of joy there was a pervading air of tragedy. The little procession stopped, mesmerized.

She looked breathtaking. Her dress was of white satin, over which cascaded tiers of Brussels lace. The collar was high and the sleeves were full-length and fitted. There was a court train falling from the shoulders in folds of billowing white and embroidered with seed pearls and silver. A wreath of orange blossoms held the tulle veil in place, and one layer was brought forward over her face and fell to her knees; not so much to follow the custom of indicating the shy, innocence of the bride, as to hide her tear-swollen eyes. Despite her own despondency, she quietly thanked them all for being there and commented on how lovely they looked.

Little did they know that the bouquet she clutched was a hastily prepared replacement for the promised one of orchids that was supposed to have arrived from Blenheim Palace.

After the initial shock, Mrs Vanderbilt bustled into activity and hastened the bridesmaids into the waiting carriages, and they began the journey to the church. May, although puzzled and disturbed, instinctively knew that in spite of all they had to carry on and execute their duties with grace.

As they processed down the aisle, through the flowers and ribbons, between the ranks of assembled guests, young as she was, she struggled with the realisation that it was a charade, despite the lovely music, the choreographed ceremony and the time-honoured words of the marriage vows.

As required by her breeding and her training, May Goelet fulfilled her role as bridesmaid as perfectly as Consuelo did that of a bride, and she took care to conceal the icy chill of premonition as she realised what her own future may hold.

She observed her mother moving so comfortably through this company with its many undercurrents, and realised for the first time that probably she too could harbour such aspirations on her behalf – but May doubted that *she* could be so ruthless.

Moreover, in her heart, she already knew that she would have more spirit than Consuelo, although, equally, she was passionately confident that she would have a powerful ally, for her father would never allow such a travesty of a marriage for his beloved daughter, whether for coronet or crown.

Chapter 2
Kelso

On the afternoon of Tuesday the 25th July, 1876, in Broxmouth Park in the town of Dunbar, on the south east coast of Scotland, a little boy was born and the celebrations of his birth resounded throughout the Scottish Borders. For this child was son and heir to the Marquis of Bowmont who was, in turn, heir to the 6th Duke of Roxburghe, whose family seat was in Floors Castle in the border town of Kelso, which nestled in the vast Roxburghe estates.

Immediately the little Lord Henry John Innes Ker was hailed as Earl of Kelso, from which title he received the familiar name by which he was to be known throughout his life, namely, *Kelso*.

Broxmouth House overlooked the bleak but beautiful North Sea, and was alternately home to the Roxburghe heir or, when required, to the Dowager Duchess. Kelso was the second child of the Marquis and his wife, Lady Anne Spencer Churchill, who was the fourth daughter of the 7th Duke of Marlborough's family of eleven.

The Roxburghe's first child was a daughter, Lady Margaret Frances Susan, and she was fourteen months older than her brother.

The moment he was born, a telegram announcing the birth

was dispatched to the boy's grandfather, who was in Norway fishing. Then others were sent, announcing the good news to Floors, and to each of the key centres on the estates, and it was met with delight everywhere. Bells were rung in the castle and from the town hall spires, and in every church.

People spilled out onto the streets, rejoicing that the future of their estate, and hence their livelihood, was thus secured. Flags and bunting appeared on shops and houses and strung across the streets in an outburst of loyal celebration. And in Kelso town square, an impromptu bonfire was lit, followed quickly by similar fires in Broxlaw Hill, Bowmont, Forest, Haddon Rig and Pinkerton Hill, all settlements in the estate, all eager to show loyalty to the boy who would one day be the Roxburghe heir and, eventually, Duke.

By the next day, not only did the celebrations continue but by now they were more organised. The bells still pealed. More decorations appeared and two whole tons of coal, a barrel of tar, and a large amount of timber were delivered into Kelso town square from the castle, and a huge fire was set to be lit at 9pm that night. Barrels of beer were provided in Kelso and in the outlying village of the estate for everyone to enjoy. Once the fires were lit, *crackers and squibs* were set off and *"in places lime-lights were used to beautiful effect"*.

Meanwhile, in both the town of Kelso and of Dunbar, a group of key civic gentlemen met for a celebratory banquet *"for the purpose of showing loyalty on this auspicious occasion"*. In Kelso, they met in the *Queen's Head Hotel*, and in Dunbar they gathered in the *St George*. At both functions, loyal toasts were proposed to H.M. the Queen; the Prince & Princess of Wales; the *lord of the manor*, namely the Duke of

Roxburghe; the Happy Parents, and finally, the baby earl.

Curiously in Kelso, a loyal rider was added saying: *"But, gentlemen, I sincerely trust that none of us at this table will be spared to see him Duke. We are entirely satisfied with our present duke and we heartily hope that he may long continue among us."*

Thus, the future duke was welcomed into the world, and although he was always known as 'Kelso', he was, in due course, christened Henry John by Reverend Robert Buchanan, in Dunbar and he spent his early years happily there in Broxmouth Park.

During those years, the little family grew. Fifteen months after Kelso, another sister, Lady Victoria, was born, and eighteen months later, yet another, who was called Lady Isobel.

Throughout this time, Kelso's grandmother, the Duchess of Roxburghe, was Lady of the Bedchamber to the Queen, and, as such, spent long periods in London or Windsor.

The duke, however began to suffer from ill health, and he was advised to travel to Italy in the hope that he would regain his strength.

Anxious that he was so far from home while unwell, the Marquis and Marchioness followed him to Naples to be with him. They stayed until the doctors pronounced him fit to travel to the more clement climate of Genoa, then they felt it opportune to begin the journey back to Scotland and their family.

But Duke James relapsed, and although there was no way of communicating with the travellers, the duchess herself was urgently summonsed from Windsor, by telegram, and was with her husband when he died. The Bowmonts arrived home to this sad news, and to the realisation that their own lives would now change forever because they were now the 7th Duke and Duchess of Roxburghe.

Young Kelso then assumed the additional titles of Lord Bowmont and Cessford, and Earl Innes.

The family moved from Broxmouth Park into Floors, a magnificent, exotic castle, which was the exuberant creation of William H. Playfair after he expanded the elegant Georgian Mansion built by Robert Adams in the 18th Century. The result was a symmetrical edifice, the roofes of which were embellished with a riot of pinnacles and cupolas, which created an effect which was both dramatic and romantic. All of this was further enhanced by its setting in acres upon acres of the most luxurious parkland and farmland, divided by the mighty River Tweed that flowed throughout and ran very close to the sweeping lawns that sloped down to its banks at the rear of the castle.

The 7th Duke, also called James, adapted quickly to his responsibilities and became a popular landlord and conscientious manager of his estates. He was a strong and very active man who loved all outdoor pursuits, particularly riding, fishing and hunting, and he was an excellent shot. He also partook in the game of curling and was a valued member of the local town team, thoroughly enjoying competing at a regional level.

Over the next five years, three more children were born; Lord Alastair, Lady Evelyn and, finally, Lord Robin.

Although Duke James expected Victorian standards of discipline and respect from his children, he really enjoyed their company and he eagerly looked forward to when he could teach Kelso, and later Alastair, the sporting skills in which he himself so rejoiced. Thus, from the earliest opportunity, Kelso learned to handle a gun and a fishing rod with competence, and to be at home in the saddle. Moreover, the joy of sportsmanship was instilled into him and it was to stay with Kelso throughout his life.

Lady Anne was Mistress of the Robes for Her Majesty throughout these years, yet she still enjoyed close contact with her offspring.

As one of the eight surviving Marlboroughs (there had been eleven), she had a keen sense of family and she always maintained close ties with her own siblings and with her husband's relatives, the Innes-Kers.

At home, hers was a practical, down-to-earth approach, which gave her children a stability that was further strengthened by the fact that she truly loved her husband, and he her.

So Kelso flourished in this secure environment and was well prepared for his departure to boarding school at Eton, at the appropriate age. He was confidently settled by the time he was eventually joined there by his brother Alastair.

But this idyllic life was not to last, because when Kelso was sixteen, his life changed forever.

*****

In the October of 1892, after the boys had returned to school for the autumn term, their father was taken ill back home in Floors. He had enjoyed a day's fishing with friends one day early in the week, and had seemed fine until they were returning home, when he admitted to feeling a little unwell. He passed it off as a mere chill, so at first no-one was concerned, but then, quite quickly, he seemed to deteriorate. Lady Anne was anxious, and despite his protestations she sent for the local doctor, a Dr Rutherford, from Kelso.

He was concerned when a day or so later there seemed to be what he described as *"an abdominal obstruction"*, and suggested to the duchess that they should call in an eminent specialist, Dr P. Heron Watson from Edinburgh.

When he examined the duke, he called in two equally celebrated colleagues who were surgeons. They delayed the decision to operate until the Saturday, by which time they felt it could wait no longer, and they set about to create an on-site emergency operating theatre in the castle. They operated without any further delay.

Lady Anne, deeply anxious, made the decision then to telegram Eton and have Kelso sent home as quickly as possible with his younger brother, perhaps intuitively, sensing that it was more serious than previously thought.

Nevertheless, at first, the duke did seem to recover from the operation, and enjoyed some relief from the pain for a short while, but then there was a setback and he began to go downhill very fast. He became visibly agitated, asking over and over again for his heir, Kelso, to be brought to him. Lady Anne comforted him as best she could, assuring him that Kelso was on his way and would be with them as soon as possible.

It was after midnight when word was brought to Lady Anne that the boys were approaching, and she left the sickroom to meet them at the door and to hustle Kelso immediately to his father's side, urgently explaining the situation.

Kelso was fazed when he entered the room; there were so many people gathered there. He saw both Grandmother Roxburghe and Grandmother Marlborough; his aunt Cornelia; Lady Wimborne and her husband; his cousins, the Marjoriebanks; his eldest sister, Margaret, and the anxious doctor, who paused, hovering over his patient with a patent look of relief when he saw the young heir arrive.

They moved back to draw Kelso to the bedside. The young man barely recognised his father. But the dying man opened his eyes and gazed hungrily at the boy as he clutched his hand.

"Thank God," he whispered fiercely, using all his strength to pull Kelso closer. He gazed into his face and said: "God bless you."

Then he sank back on his pillows.

The doctor leaned over his patient and turned and looked hard at Lady Anne. She nodded her head ever so slightly and went to the door to send a waiting servant to tell the nanny to bring the other children immediately.

Lady Margaret crossed the room to put her arm round her mother, as the frightened huddle of sisters and brothers crept in.

Young Robin, at age seven too little to understand the gravity of the situation, was rubbing his eyes and protesting loudly that he'd already wished Papa goodnight and it wasn't morning yet. As they hushed him, the doctor examined their father once more, then turned sadly to Lady Anne to indicate it was all over.

Young Henry John, Earl of Kelso, bowed his head over his father's hand, still in his, and wept, realising in his intense grief that at this heartbreaking moment, that not only had he lost the father he adored, but that now his boyhood was over. At sixteen years of age, he was to assume the responsibilities of the duty conferred on him by birth. He had just become the 8th Duke of Roxburghe, and at that moment he would have given anything to have turned the clock back to the carefree years of childhood.

Over the following days, Kelso had to adapt to his change in status, both in the castle and within the family. The hardest moment was when his mother consulted *him* over the arrangements for the funeral.

In confusion and embarrassment, he begged her to make what decisions she felt best for herself, the children, and for what she felt the late duke would have wished.

Without further fuss, she told him that her real desire would be a break with family tradition. Whereas all previous dukes had been buried at Bowden crypt, she would prefer her husband buried in Kelso Abbey. She explained to her son that his father had been so popular with the tenants and the townsfolk, that it would give them a chance join the funeral procession to show their respects should they so wish. Naturally, there would be representatives from all the noble families and all the important people from the area, but she felt that he would have liked the ordinary folk to feel a part of it too.

Nevertheless, she did decide to follow the current Victorian custom and that the womenfolk, herself included, would not attend the internment. Instead, she would prefer a simple, private service for immediate family and close friends, at home in Floors. Then Kelso would assume his responsibility as heir and lead the mourners.

Kelso readily agreed. So, on the appointed day, he stood beside his mother in the ante-room to the dining room, where his father's body was lying in state, and he solemnly welcomed the guests as they filed in to say their final farewells.

Reverend J. Gordon Napier of Kelso, and Reverend Mr Buchanan from Dunbar, conducted the service, then the eight men who had been chosen to represent each aspect of estate service stepped forward to bear the coffin to the waiting hearse.

There was James Wilson, a farm servant; William Rutherford, a shepherd; George Turnbull, a blacksmith; Oliver Wright, a joiner; Robert Hyslop, a hedger; Walter Burns, a carter, and John Aichison and Thomas Reid, who were both foresters.

The heavily-draped carriage, with its black, plumed horses stood under the great stone portico as the coffin was laid in the swathes of black crepe.

Then the many wreathes were banked around it. On the top was laid one from Queen Victoria, with a card that read: *As a mark of sincere regard, Victoria R.1*; Lady Anne's wreath, with its poignant message: *From your loving, broken-hearted widow*; there was one from the children, signed by each with their family pet names: *Margie, Kelso, Via, Isabel, Alastair, Evelyn and Robin*; and finally, the one from the Prince and Princess of Wales in the shape of a white heart, with the inscription: *As a token of sincere friendship and regard.*

As chief mourner, Kelso travelled in the coach behind the

hearse with young Alastair, who was nearly twelve years old. The coach behind them carried Sir John Cowell, who was there representing her Majesty the Queen. Behind him rode their uncle, Lord Charles Innes-Ker, with his sons and their cousin, Sir George Grant Suttie. The next five carriages carried relations and close family friends, behind which drove a long line of coaches with mourners from all over the county and beyond.

The procession wound its way slowly down the tree-lined avenue and out of the gates into Kelso itself. Every shop was closed and each household had curtains tightly drawn as a mark of respect. Silent crowds lined the streets, their heads bowed and the men clutching their caps.

Eventually the cortege drew up at the abbey gates. A silent crowd had already gathered at a discreet distance to watch the proceedings, as Lady Anne had expected.

The eight bearers lifted the coffin out and carried it into the churchyard, where, after an impressive but short prayer service, Kelso and Alastair took up their positions as pallbearers; Kelso at the head; Lord Alasdair, Mr Marjoriebanks and Lord de Ramsay on the left side of the coffin with Lord Charles, Lord Kensington and Lord Curzon on the right. Sir George Grant Suttie stood at the feet.

Then the remains were lowered into the grave, which was decorated with ivy, moss and white flowers.

In the weeks after the funeral, the decision was made that Kelso should return to his education, as his father had desired, and that he should go on to Sandhurst, the Military Academy, to train to become an officer in the Royal Lifeguards, known proudly as the Royal Blues. This was the family tradition, and

Lady Anne was determined that he should not be prevented from doing so. She was confident that she could efficiently manage the estates, with the advice and guidance of their trusted factor and the rest of the staff, until Kelso came of age, and she also devoted herself to being parent to all seven children.

In due course therefore, Kelso was gazetted as a lieutenant in the Blues in the summer of 1867 and sent into service in the House of the Prince of Wales.

Nevertheless, the young duke was always aware of the responsibilities of his calling, and those towards his siblings. Moreover, the high regard he developed over these years for his mother's intelligence, competence and wisdom was to give him a perspective on women's capabilities, which was to build in him a great respect. He was repelled by the superficiality of the frivolities of the late Victorian and Edwardian scene, and the levity with which so many of his peers regarded marriage, which was so far from what he had experienced with his parents. He hated and avoided fashionable courtship routines being enacted all around him, so that never would he be seen jostling in some nuptial carousel to satisfy the naked ambitions of mammas eager to purchase a coronet for their offspring.

Chapter 3
Jubilee

In 1897, Queen Victoria celebrated her Diamond Jubilee, having reigned for sixty years, and the sparkling round of delights that were designed for that summer were to outshine all that went before.

Everyone with a claim to social position, either by birth or wealth, flocked to London in unprecedented numbers from Europe and America for *The Season*.

Inevitably, the Goelets crossed the Atlantic in their new yacht, *The Mayflower*, which they had recently commissioned from shipbuilders in Clydebank, Scotland, and which they had named in honour of their daughter, May.

They rented Wimborne House, an elegant residence in the most fashionable area of London so that they could attend and host functions throughout *The Season*. And this was to be the season of all seasons, as London, along with the whole of Britain, feted their aged Queen. The many years of austerity caused by Victoria's morosely extended mourning for her late husband, Albert, who by now had been thirty-six years dead, seemed to visibly lift as rich and poor were determined to celebrate.

Ogden Goelet and his wife, Mary, had been regulars on both the London and the European scene for many years. But by these latter years of the century, Ogden's health was failing and his doctors recommended that he should spend even more time in Europe, as a result of which the Goelets became even more integrated into the *elite set*, and socialized on a regular basis with the Prince of Wales, around whom buzzed the heart of Society.

May celebrated her seventeenth birthday on October 6th 1897, and, although she had not yet made her debut back home in the States, she was invited to be presented to the British Court at the debutante's Ball in Buckingham Palace on Friday, 4th May, which that year was to be held early in the London Spring Season, so as to be well in time for May and all the other young debutantes to be included on the invitation list of the many Jubilee functions. This was what Mrs Goelet had dreamed and planned for her only daughter ever since Consuelo's marriage; but the timing, which, incredibly, was beyond her control, was absolute perfection. What better time for her to seek out an eligible aristocratic husband for May than when *everyone* who was *anyone* was in London to honour the Queen?

Naturally, Consuelo, as Duchess of Marlborough, was in town for the coming festivities, and Mrs Goelet, calling on their relationship and long-time friendship, invited her to lunch with May on both the Wednesday and Thursday of that week. Who better was there to groom her young cousin for her big occasion?

For Consuelo, herself an American, had been presented at court when little older than May, although by then she was a bride and a duchess.

Naturally, the ambitious mother had no idea that life was already intolerable for Consuelo, who, now her fortune had stabilized the Marlborough finances and she had succeeded in producing the required heir and second son, was bitterly isolated because the duke no longer made any pretence of needing her except in a formal and decorative capacity in public.

With a sick heart, Consuelo kept up appearances and obliged, even though she knew from experience the motivating force behind Mrs Goelet's apparently innocent agenda was to select a *suitable* husband for May.

Nevertheless, she would not disillusion a seventeen-year-old girl on the eve of so momentous an occasion, for to be presented before Queen Victoria and thereby step into adult Society was an exciting rite of passage for any well-born young lady. Hence, Consuelo suppressed any feeling of doubt on May's behalf, and threw herself into advising and encouraging her to such a degree that May anticipated her entrance onto the world stage with unspoilt delight.

So it was that Ogden and Mary Goelet watched with pride as their only daughter was graciously received by Queen Victoria herself in her Jubilee year.

Mrs Goelet did not doubt for one minute that May would create a stir in society and not only because of her vast inheritance but because she was actually quite beautiful. She was petite in build and a brunette, and her vivid colouring was matched with an assured presence and a keen wit. Moreover, she was highly intelligent, with a passionate and informed interest in the arts. Already, like her father, she loved ancient medieval tapestries, which she too was to collect one day. In her own right, she was developing a keen appreciation for contemporary evolving art movements, particularly those in

France. As a rich young American lady, she was well-travelled, and had grown up on the international scene, which had offered her a more cosmopolitan education than many of her sisters among young aristocratic British ladies; together with an independence in spirit, which was quite unusual and therefore refreshingly exciting.

Inevitably, the big occasion passed off with style and, with May now a fully-fledged debutante, the mother and daughter awaited, with great anticipation, the official launch of celebrations which was to be the Jubilee Procession on the 22nd June – but each for for different reasons.

The day dawned, bright and warm, and the Goelets took their carriage to join their friend, Mrs Bentnick, to take up a vantage point from which to see the great procession. All London was en fete, and excited people thronged the whole route.

Indeed, a few days beforehand, when the Queen had made the overnight journey from Balmoral, Scotland, in the royal train, groups of loyal subjects had gathered on stations throughout Britain to stand in silence and bare their heads in homage as the sleeping monarch passed through.

London was bedecked in flags and bunting, with luxurious garlands festooning every lamp-post, archway and any other available space; and, for the privileged, there were banks of seating erected at vantage points. One firm actually pulled down an entire shop to provide such seating in St Paul's Churchyard, much to the bemusement of locals, summed up in a cartoon in *Punch*, which showed a colonial visitor scratching his head and asking if they planned to pull down St Paul's itself for the occasion!

When the royal carriage came in sight, it was drawn by eight cream horses and flanked by outriders from both Regiments of the Household Cavalry, Kelso's Blues and Royals, and the Life Guards.

Ahead of this rode one young officer from the Life Guards, who had been chosen to lead the whole procession because of his outstanding good looks. His name was Captain Oswald Ames, and the Prince of Wales himself had invited him on behalf of his mother to perform this duty. Reports claimed that he bashfully tried to refuse the honour, but that the prince insisted. It is fairly certain that he caught May's eye that day, but although she may have appreciated his exceedingly glamourous appearance, little could she guess that he would be a significant figure in her life a year or two later!

Behind them came all the royal pageantry that made the occasion unforgettable. First there were the carriages of the other Royal family members present and their guests. For Victoria's children alone to be in attendance meant that most European Royal Houses were represented, but the Queen had decided that this celebration, unlike her Golden Jubilee, which was celebrated by all the Crown Heads of Europe, was to be far more representative of the Commonwealth alone.

Hence, the eleven Colonial Prime Ministers were in attendance plus the important leaders of her Empire, together with delegates from those who were in Commonwealth service on land or sea.

This made a very colourful and vital asset to the procession as each regiment of the Army and Navy, from both Britain and the Colonies, paraded, all bands playing. And wherever they passed, the crowds erupted in fervent and very vocal expressions of loyalty.

When the royal carriage passed, the cheering was so great that the Queen wrote in her journal later that night:

'No-one ever, I believe, has met with such an ovation as was given to me, passing those six miles of streets... the cheering was quite deafening and every face seemed to be filled with real joy. I was much moved and gratified.'

The procession progressed slowly to the great Cathedral of Saint Paul's, where a Thanksgiving Service was to be conducted.

Due to the Queen's lameness and frailty, there had been much discussion as to how it could be achieved, as the great flight of steps to the entrance presented such a problem.

One idea had been that the carriage should be drawn by men into the church and up the aisle, but logistically this was not realistic. Then it was decided that the Archbishop would come out and stand on the steps to conduct the service, surrounded by the other bishops (over a hundred in all), other members of the clergy, the massed choirs and the Gentlemen-at-Arms.

As the Queen's coach arrived, the whole throng was assembled, waiting on the steps, and the choir sang the Te Deum, followed by the Lord's Prayer '*most beautifully chanted*', after which the Archbishop conducted, as instructed by Her Majesty, a *short* service, while she sat comfortably and regally in the carriage.

Gathered around were the selected guests who would have formed the congregation within. Here, the Goelets participated and enjoyed the spectacle in genteel comfort, away from the exuberance of the crowds.

When it was over, the procession continued via the Mansion House and through South London before returning over Westminster Bridge, past the Houses of Parliament to Buckingham Palace.

For May, the next big event was to be the following Monday, the 22nd of June, for this was to be her first royal Garden Party.

After spending the weekend on board the *Mayflower*, the family returned to Wimborne House to prepare. Mrs Goelet, remembering the charming effect of May's bridesmaid's outfit at the Marlborough wedding, selected a similar gown in white with a blue sash and a delightful picture hat, circled with lush roses. She was delighted with the effect, and the proud parents escorted their daughter to the first of many parties at Buckingham Palace.

To her mother's delight, May's arrival caused the hoped for response. Young men of all ranks gathered round, displaying perfect etiquette and courtesy, but nevertheless showing excitement at the attractive challenge before them.

May, delighted as any seventeen year old would be, lapped up the compliments and the requests to receive house-calls, and enjoyed the flowery promises to fill her card with partners at her first ball. Naturally, all of this was chaperoned by her ecstatic mother, who beamed down on the courtly throng, already hearing wedding bells within the year.

This is where Kelso will have had his first proper sighting of Miss May Goelet, for at this time he was, as an officer in the Blues, in the service of the Prince of Wales, and would be either on duty or socializing himself with the other guests. But to May, he was just another delightful gentleman in the galaxy establishing orbit around her.

In all this excitement, however, there was one function which loomed larger in her calendar than even a Royal Garden Party, and that was Lady Devonshire's Jubilee Ball. It was to be held on 3rd July, and was already rumoured to be the greatest and most exotic event for this whole season, if not in recent history – exclusively for the *'inner circle of Society'*. Reports of the preparations alone predicted that it would outshine, if not eclipse, all the official celebrations put together. And, already, each tailor and seamstress was totally booked out and every theatrical costumier's resources were stretched to the limit.

An unprecedented number of noble visitors spent hours in art galleries and great houses, poring over portraits of great figures from the past – or, rather, how they were attired. It was even whispered that members of the Royal family were surreptitiously approached for the loan of priceless items of jewelry or militaria to complement exotic outfits.

For this was to be a themed fancy dress ball for which the invitations stated that guests were to present themselves at Devonshire House at 10.30pm dressed *'in an allegorical or historical costume, dated earlier than 1820'*. So, all 700 guests vied to achieve the finest and most authentic outfits. It was themed in periods, and thus *'divided into Courts'*, presided over by various leading aristocratic ladies, who were *'attended by their friends as princes and courtiers'*.

The four principal 'Courts' were the British Elizabethan Court, the French Court of Louis XV & XVI, the Russian Court of Catherine II, plus the Oriental Court.

The Elizabethan Court was presided over by Lady

Tweedmouth, an Aunt of Kelso's, dressed as Queen Elizabeth I, and her friends depicted the well-known characters of that period.

Lady Curzon was dressed as Queen Marie Leczinska, and Lady Warwick was Marie Antoinette, and together they led the French Court.

Lady Raincliffe led the Court of the Empress Catherine the Great of Russia. Finally, the hostess, Lady Devonshire led the Oriental Court, herself exotically dressed as Zenobia, the 3rd Century warrior queen of Palmyra.

In addition to these, there was the Italian Court, led by the Countess of Kellie and Mar, while Lord Latham led an independent Venetian Court and Lady Ormonde, as Queen Guinevere led the Knights of the Round Table.

The costumes were sumptuous, executed in the richest silks, velvets and tissued silvers and golds and most were encrusted with jewels.

The host, the Duke of Devonshire, was splendidly attired as the Emperor Charles V, whose family, the Hapsburgs, he uncannily resembled. He wore an outfit copied from a portrait, and set off by a genuine and priceless collar and badge of the Golden Fleece, loaned to him by the Prince of Wales for the occasion.

May joined Lady Grosvenor, a Miss West and Miss Oppenheim as ladies in attendance on Princess Daisy of Pless in her Oriental Court. The princess played the part of the Queen of Sheba (one of several as it happens), and she was photographed for the famous Lafayette Studio Collection the next day and her sumptuous costume described in detail in the Daily Telegraph July 3rd 1897 as follows: *[She wore] 'a dress of purple and gold shot gauze. The bodice, the skirt nearly to the waist, and the train was one mass of jewels, thickly encrusted medallions of raised gold. Turquoise, bearing hieroglyphics, bore a prominent part in the designs, which included yellow, red, purple, green, blue and white stones. There was a sash of cloth of gold, also jewelled superbly, and the Assyrian badge worn in front of the bodice at the waistline. An Assyrian headdress, with jewels on either ear, and a high, jewelled, stiff feather, and chains of turquoise worn slung on either arm, from shoulder to wrist, completed a costume of the utmost magnificence.'.*

May was pictured in the studio reclining on a thick velvet pillow on a silk-draped chaise-longue, resting her head on her arm. Her dress, with a wide-embroidered neckline, was of a soft, flowing silk, caught in at the waist by a gold belt. The sleeves were minimal caps and over her left shoulder there was a gathered swathe of silk, tied in a knot at the waist and fanned out to display the exquisite and embroidered and deep ends of the sash so that the top layer ended before the decoration on the under level began. Both ends were finished off with finely worked lace. The skirt below was embroidered with a delicate border of wild flowers that formed an undulating pattern. All the needlework showed metallic threads and small jewels.

On her head there was an exotic headdress that was part turban, but the crown swept up into a cone shape from which stood a large ostrich feather. The headdress was decorated in silks, ribbons and jewels, the principal of which was a central large stone from which hung a gem set in a decorated gold-worked pendant, which hung down from her forehead. Around her throat there was a heavy two-tiered neclace and her arms were adorned with bangles.

The Duchess of Devonshire, Queen of the Oriental Court, was exotically dressed in her persona as Zenobia, Queen of Palmyra. Her dress, of gold tissue, was exquisitely embroidered in gold and encrusted with diamonds, rubies and emeralds, and a beautiful peacock was embroidered in gold and gems down the front panel of the skirt. Glittering stars were '*scattered*' overall, and her emerald-green train was also embroidered in precious stones.

Kelso was definitely on the guest list, but he characteristically avoided the attention of the eager reporters from *The Times* and other journals. He was not listed in any of the four principal *courts*, so presumably he chose something less ostentatious, and probably military. But his mother, Lady Anne, Dowager Duchess of Roxburghe, a lady of the Royal Bedchamber at this period, was with her sister, Lady Tweedmouth in the Elizabethan Court.

She was dressed as Bess of Hardwicke *'in a beautiful Elizabethan costume in black velvet with a white satin front, embroidered with pearls, pointed bodice, jewelled girdle, and lace ruff, the big satin sleeves were inserted with white satin squares edged with pearls, and the black velvet cap and tulle veil were bordered with the same. 'The Morning Post, 3rd July 1897.* She was photographed on 2nd July, on the day of the Ball, at Devonshire House. Lady Tweedmouth was Queen Elizabeth and her husband was Lord Dudley.

The Royal party entered well into the spirit of the evening. The Prince of Wales was dressed in black velvet and silver-grey silk, richly embroidered in steel-gold and jet, as the Grand Master of the Knights Hospitaller of Malta. Alexandra,

Princess of Wales was dressed as Marguerite de Valois, in a gown of creamy white, encrusted with diamonds and pearls and she wore a high choker of pearls around her neck.

The Duke of York went as an Elizabethan, George Clifford, the Queen's Champion, and his wife, Mary, was in pale blue satin, embroidered in pearls and silver as a lady of the court of Marguerite de Valois.

The invitations were for 10.30pm, and the glittering guests arrived early, eager not to miss anything. The whole of the first floor of Devonshire House had been turned over to the festivities, including the usually private rooms of their hosts, which were converted into saloons at each end of the building. A dais had been erected in the first room off the stair for the Royal party to sit and receive the colourful company. A large marquee, or *'supper tent'*, had been erected in the garden, decorated by three fine old Louis XIVth tapestries, and it was accessed by a temporary staircase from the first floor of the house.

Electric lights were subtly hung within garlands of flowers to light the tent, but as carefully concealed as possible while still illuminating the scene. Nothing else *modern* was allowed, and every musician, footman, servant, herald and waiting maid – even in the ladies' cloakroom – was dressed in pre-19^{th}century costume.

The National Anthem at 11pm announced the arrival of the Royal party, who took their seats on the dais as the grand company processed before them in their courtly groupings.

This over, the quadrilles began, in very stately fashion, their slow grandeur, perfectly showcasing the magnificent costumes of the entire assembly.

Waltzes followed for those described by the Times as *'young and energetic enough to dance!'*. More mature and less energetic ones sauntered in the garden, which was ablaze with fairy lights. Supper in the tent followed, and the revellers did not disperse until almost dawn.

Despite the excitement and exertions of the night before, the full social round continued, more so than previously, after the exchange of invitations and visiting cards. May had a luncheon appointment with a friend, Katherine, followed by a dinner appointment at 8.15 in the evening with the Earl and Countess of Pembroke.

Two days later, she escorted her parents to a dinner party in Chesterfield Gardens to meet His Royal Highness and the Duke and Duchess of Saxe-Coburg, after which she went on to the Savoy Hotel for Lady Moreton's dance.

One of the young gentlemen who was particularly captivated by May during these entertainments was the young Duke of Manchester, and his name appears in her engagement diary for Wednesday 7th noting that he was her escort at Lords cricket ground. It is certain that he also sought her out on that Friday evening at the ball at Stafford House, home of the Duchess of Sutherland.

To everyone's horror, on the following day there was an article in the *Times*, claiming that Miss May Goelet was engaged to the Duke of Manchester.

Ogden Goelet was absolutely furious. The young Duke had made no attempt to follow the rules of etiquette and approach him regarding a possible engagement. Besides, May had made her debut barely five weeks before – and not at all in America yet. There was no way he – or anybody - could be considered as a possible suitor so early in her social career.

May had indeed met William Angus Drogo Montagu, the 9th Duke of Manchester, familiarly called Kim, and some of his family.

In fact, the Goelets recalled that back in June she had accompanied the young man's mother, the duchess, to the theatre to see *Secret Service*. Goelet was worldly enough to realize that old and infirm Consuelo Yznaga, herself an American (after whom Consuelo Vanderbilt had been named) was looking for the best – and richest – bride for her son. It was public knowledge that the Manchesters were exceedingly poor and that their home, Kimbolton Castle, was in desperate need of repair. At this time, Kim was barely twenty years old and had inherited his father's phenomenal debts five years previously, at the tender age of fifteen.

Nevertheless, the fact that poverty was motivating this young man to court his beloved daughter was infuriating enough to Ogden, but, the knowledge that not only had the young duke already had a rakish reputation with the ladies, and had also previously, falsely declared himself engaged to Pauline Astor, put him way beyond any chance of consideration.

The tone of the headlines in the *Times* and the *New York Journal* claiming '*Another duchess for America*' and '*A Great surprise in Social Circles*' further exacerbated Ogden's opposition, and without delay he summonsed the London representative from the *New York Journal* to Wimborne House to categorically refute the whole story.

He demanded that it should be printed as soon as possible, on both sides of the Atlantic, and that it should clearly state that his daughter was not, and would not be, announcing any engagement in the near future. He further made it clear that it was his wish that May would *not* be considering a European aristocrat as a prospective husband at all, but that she would seek for a suitor a good American '*like herself*', one who was responsible for contributing to, and handling his own independent fortune.

With so forceful and public a declaration, Mrs Goelet had no choice, for the present, but to harbour secretly the plans she had no intention abandoning. She continued to foster friendships with the many mammas and even older sisters of potential hopefuls for the future, when, she was confident, she could urge her husband to come around to her way of thinking.

Hence, the season continued and May went to the theatre, house-concerts, balls, dinners and mixed with all the right people. And, once again, she was invited to dine with the Prince of Wales, meeting up with his inner circle and inevitably the members of his suite. But it was Kelso's great friend, Lord Crichton, who made the first move to become acquainted with May at this period, probably because of the distaste Kelso felt for the marriage-politics game.

Cricton invited May to spend the afternoon with his family at the Guards' Regatta, and to join them later for dinner. May had inherited her father's love of boats and boating, so she was delighted and it was a refreshing interlude. She discovered that she shared much in common with the Crichtons and the young viscount was exceedingly handsome and dashing, and great fun to be with.

His family, while welcoming this potential connection, were not inclined in any way to pursue it aggressively. Hence,

Ogden Goelet felt comfortable accepting their invitation to lunch on the following Tuesday.

The Crichtons were the family of the 4th Earl of Erne, from Crom Castle in Fermanagh, Northern Ireland. Their eldest son was indeed attracted to May but realized that this was not the time to make any such declaration so soon after the fiasco over the Duke of Manchester.

Instead, he developed a firm friendship with the young lady that was to last for many years. Perhaps he did, however, confide his feelings for May to Kelso, his close friend, because it is certain that the latter made no attempt to approach May throughout the period that Crichton was a possible suitor.

As they drew towards the end of July the Season quietened down a little. The Goelet family went on board the *Mayflower* to head for Cowes to enjoy the most renowned sailing event of the year.

Cowes is a seaport on the Isle of Wight, lying due south of the port of Southampton, England. It sits on the west bank of the mouth of the River Medina, and faces the smaller town of East Cowes. It is famous for sailing, and Cowes Castle is home to the Royal Yacht Squad, which ranks first among the world's most elite yachting clubs. During the first week of August every year, Cowes hosts the world's oldest and most prestigious Regatta, an event which would have been the high point of Ogden's British Season.

Cowes itself is also famed for Osborne House, which was Queen Victoria's favourite summer residence since she and her husband, Prince Albert, had bought it with her own private funds and the proceeds from the sale of Brighton Pavilion, where earlier monarchs had taken their holidays. But Victoria had felt that too accessible to the press and the public when she wanted privacy for herself and her family. The house itself in Cowes was planned and designed by Prince Albert, using the new technological skills of prefabrication to speed up the process. He himself had designed the grounds, so there Victoria not only enjoyed privacy, but always felt a sense of closeness to her beloved Albert. And it was to be there, in Osborne House, that she was to die in 1901.

In addition during this particular year of Victoria's Diamond Jubilee, the Isle of Wight attained a third reason for fame, as it was the place from where Marconi had succeeded in setting up the world's first radio at a tiny shed at the *Needles Battery*, which is situated at the western tip of the island.

The Queen had immediately realized its potential and actually used the technology on the morning of the great procession, to send a message to her people. Later that evening she recorded in her diary that before she left Buckingham Palace she touched an electric button, *"by which I started a message which was telegraphed throughout the whole Empire... From my heart I thank my beloved people. May God bless them."* Victoria's diary *Victoria* – Mullens & Munsen.

Each day of that August week, the Goelets again enjoyed the company of Europe's most glittering. On the Monday, the Prince of Wales came on board to visit them. The following day, the King of the Belgians visited the yacht.

On the Wednesday, they lunched on Wolverton's Yacht, and they had lunch with Lady Randolph on the Thursday. Then, on Friday afternoon, they hosted the Princess of Wales with the Empress Eugenie.

That night, the festivities of the week were rounded off

with a spectacular firework party.

Once the Regatta was over, they returned to the mainland to join friends as house-guests at a country house called Knightscroft. A few days later, on August 12th, they moved on to Highcliffe Castle in Christchurch. The castle had been rebuilt in the 1830s by Charles, Lord Stuart de Rothsay, from stones which had been brought over from France in twelve barges. The stones had been purchased from the ruined Benedictine Abbey at Jumiege and the Grande Maison des Andelys, and shipped to a bay known originally as *Lord Bute's Gap* but its name was changed to *Steamer Point* when a steamer ran aground there and was subsequently used as accommodation for the builders.

The castle was a romantic, L-shaped building, positioned so that the oriole window on the south eastern face overlooked the magnificent view across Christchurch Bay and the Solent to the Needles in the Isle of Wight.

But, during these days, Ogden's health was beginning to cause concern, and although he did not wish to curtail their visit, on the 19th August, to his relief, May and her mother did accompany him back to *The Mayflower* and they returned to Cowes. Once there, it became apparent that he was fading rapidly, and he died on 27th August, on board his beloved yacht, plunging his family into the deepest mourning.

Chapter Four
1898 - 1899 The Marriage-go-round

In June of 1898, after a full period of mourning for her father, May and her mother returned briefly to London.

With Ogden dead, Mrs Goelet saw herself now free to pursue *her* ambitions for May without restraint. In fairness to her, she genuinely believed that she was creating the ideal future for her daughter, and set herself to facilitate its realization.

May, on the other hand, had no desire to be married off to anyone, although she delighted in all the attention. She was shrewd enough to know that her vast fortune was a greater attraction to many of her apparently ardent suitors than herself and called on her youth and inexperience to avoid any form of commitment.

Nevertheless, she was constantly escorted by eligible bachelors from all over Europe as she lunched, dined and danced, always strictly chaperoned by her mother or another reputable matron. Although they were to return to the States in July, the mothers and sisters of several young gentlemen sought the friendship of a more than willing Mrs Goelet, and showered them both with invitations for the autumn through to winter, several of them for house parties.

Thus, on their departure in July, the press bewailed that May retuned to the States still 'Mistress of her heart', but they commented that a flurry of young hopefuls made a trip Stateside at just the same time as the Goelets. One can surmise that the most influential enjoyed some of Mrs Goelet's legendary hospitality in Ochre Court, their summer mansion in Rhode Island – as indeed did the American friends, several of whom also sought the hand of the lovely Miss May Goelet.

Still, she was unpromised when they returned in early September to Wimborne House. Then, after attending the theatre on three consecutive nights, May and her mother set off for Ireland on Friday 9th to visit Crom Castle and the Crichtons for two whole weeks.

Crom Castle was built on the upper shores of Lough Erne, in County Fermanagh.

Surrounded by the waters of Lough Erne, it sat in the almost 2,000 acre estate with elegant parkland, a spectacular oak wood, a deer-park, and acres of lush pasture land. There was also a Victorian boathouse, which was the first Lough Erne Yacht Club House from which the gentlemen took their sport, watched by the picnicking ladies and from which, also, the gentlemen took their lady guests for leisurely boating on the lough.

May loved her visit to Crom and became very fond of Lady Erne, who in turn was delighted with her young guest.

Crighton was undoubtedly captivated by now, and the two mothers decided not to interfere, but to let matters take their course. This left May free to enjoy the visit and to enjoy a genuine friendship with Crichton, despite his occasional declarations of love. She managed to convince him of her true affection without giving him the impression that there was any underlying promise of love. He responded with gallant attention, jovial enjoyment in their shared activities, and sometimes a casual, if dramatic reference to his broken heart.

The fortnight passed and the Goelets left Ireland, and although there was no admission of a romance between them, Crichton was to be May's frequent escort in London that season.

But May and her mother did not travel directly back to London. They went first to Lord Savile's home in Nottinghamshire, Rufford Abbey, for a couple of days, and then travelled up to Fifeshire, in Scotland, to Alloa House, to the estate of the Countess of Mar and Kellie.

The Countess was young and extremely beautiful, and she was sister to the Earl of Shaftesbury, who was thirty years old, unmarried and causing his family endless anxiety.

She longed to encourage him to marry a respectable, and preferably wealthy young lady, who would give him stability and hopefully, a sense of responsibility. He, himself, had little desire to settle down. Worse than that, he had a penchant for ladies of the theatre!

Two years beforehand, when he was an aide-de-camp to Lord Brassey in Australia, he had caused a huge scandal by falling in love with a Chicago soubrette, called Sadie McDonald, whom he had first seen on stage in *A Trip to Chinatown*.

So infatuated had he been that he had given her £50,000 worth of jewelry and proposed to her. To the undeniable relief of his family and friends, the poor lady died before the proposed marriage came about but the bereaved young earl sought solace in the company of his other theatrical friends.

Whether or not the countess really believed that May would for one moment consider a gentleman with such a history, despite his title, is not clear; but, in reality, there was definitely no chance when she had the choice of Europe's most eligible at her feet.

Moreover, to a girl of 19, a man of 30 seemed very old. Nevertheless, back in London later that year, his name occasionally appeared in May's diary in a theatre group or card game, or even at dinner engagements, but never as May's actual escort.

Once again, May and her mother returned to London where the season had died down and they enjoyed a less hectic programme of afternoon teas, and theatre trips preceded by dinner at *Prince's*. Prince's Hall was an exclusive and expensive restaurant in Piccadilly, much frequented by the wealthy en route to the theatre. The ceiling of the 'grand salon' was decorated throughout with heavy white mouldings, picked out in gold against brick-red panels *'powdered with gold fleur de lys and palms filling the corner'*. The hall itself was bright with mirrors and screens decorated with flowers. It was brilliantly lit with electric lights, and clusters of electric candles stood on every table. Over the entrance to the kitchen there was a *'white railed musicians' gallery'*, and each musician employed there was claimed to be *'a soloist of some celebrit'*. The manager at that time, a Mr Fourault, boasted widely of his beautiful kitchen and how *'to avoid draughts in lifts'*, all dishes were carried by hand directly to his guests. (The Victorian Dictionary)

May also had tea at Hyde Park Barracks with Crichton; he

partnered her to the theatre and she met him at the *Supper Club*, among other partners less worthy of note.

Skating seemed to be the fashionable mode of exercise that season, and May took every opportunity to partake in the sport.

In October, they went back to Scotland for a week to visit the Duke and Duchess of Buccleugh and Queensbury at Drumlanrig Castle, which was set on a hill, overlooking Nithsdale and the River Nith. The romantic and beautiful sandstone castle, built in the *grand manner* stood in vast acres of park and forest land, and by this period had beautifully laid out Victorian-style gardens, which were much admired by their guests.

The quiet time of the season passed off with the usual activities in London and a couple more visits to country houses throughout November. A couple of evenings were spent with Crichton's mother, Lady Erne, at the theatre or the *Supper Club*, but little more appears in May's engagement diary until they left for Wilton House on December 4th.

Wilton was the family seat of the Earl and Countess of Pembroke, brother and sister-in-law of May's aunt Belle. To May, it was very much a family home, and Lord Sydney Herbert, the 14th Earl, and his wife, Lady Beatrice, welcomed them warmly as family. Their eldest son, Reginald Herbert, was the same age as May, and treated her in a brotherly fashion although they were only very distant cousins. This meant that times spent at Wilton were away from the immediate pressures of being pursued as a possible bride, although several of Lord Herbert's friends did join them throughout the holiday season.

One, Lord Ingestre, was to become interested in May at

this point, but he did not press his suit until the following year, for May, who was determined not to allow this time to be spoilt, treated them all alike and spent her time skating, walking, riding and driving out; in fact, generally having a good time.

It seemed that her mother, too, was relaxed at Wilton, and was satisfied to allow things to take a natural course, provided May was seen to be suitably chaperoned albeit less rigorously than in London.

This welcome respite lasted into January, with brief visits to other homes but with Wilton as their base.

No sooner had they left in mid-January, however, than the most extraordinary bid was made for the hand of Miss May Goelet. And apparently the plan was three years in preparation!

A fifty-year-old widowed German Prince, Hugo von Hohenlohe, had observed May and her fortune from afar, and had set the wheels in motion for what he thought was a subtle way to present his suit to the young lady's mother. He employed an agent in London, a Captain Ladestas de Portenoy, former military attaché to the German Embassy in London, agreeing to pay $10,000 if consideration of his marriage proposal was secured.

The captain thought that the wisest way of approaching the matter, was to employ a London solicitor, Lucius O'Brien, as his assistant. They decided to enlist the help of a couple of ladies who moved in May's circle, having first of all won their confidence by giving generous gifts to her favourite charity.

So in January, as the Goelets returned from Wilton, the lady visited Mrs Goelet with the proposal. The next day she wrote to the agent from Belgrave Square, saying:

Dear Sir,

I saw Mrs Goelet yesterday and she begged me to say how flattered she felt at the proposal with regard to Prince Hohenlohe, but that her daughter was still very young, and as she had never seen him she must decline the proposal. Should they meet hereafter it would be a different matter, but without any personal knowledge on either side the thing would be impossible.

She added:

Miss Goelet is a charming girl in every way but is very English in her feelings and views and dislikes the 'mariage de convenance' system abroad extremely. I do not think she will ever marry unless she falls in love with a man.

Several days later, this lady discovered for the first time that Prince Hugo was fifty, and she hastily penned another letter saying that in all honesty she believed that May would never consider this proposal at all on account of his age.

But Prince Hugo was persistent and tried to arrange an appointment to meet May, who refused.

With wounded pride, Hohenlohe returned to Berlin but failed to pay his agent meanwhile. After numerous unsuccessful attempts to recover his fee, de Porkoney brought a legal suit against the prince and scandal was averted, only because Hugo's aunt paid several hundred pounds to settle the claim.

Unpeturbed, the elderly suitor followed the Goelets to America in his attempt to meet May, and was even entertained by the Vanderbilts. May, however, remained resolute, and, in this case, she was fully supported by her mother.

Perhaps to reaffirm her preference for *young* men, and feeling safe with the Crichtons, May agreed to attend a cotillion with Lord Crichton in January, and she accompanied his parents, the Ernes, to dinner. This was followed by joining them for both days of the the Grand Miltary Steeplechase in March. But, as her mother hosted the Prince of Wales for the last time before returning with May to the States, she little realized that someone had at last caught May's eye.

May Goelet was infatuated, or perhaps she had finally fallen in love. But she kept her feelings very much to herself during her time in America, certain that her mother would not favour her choice.

Naturally, she found the long separation intolerable, and she longed to return to the gentleman of her affection as quickly as possible.

When at last she arrived at Wimbone House on May 30th, May wrote in capital letters in her appointment diary 'ARRIVED'. But, to May's horror, and before she could break the news to her mother, they were met by a report blazoned all over the press that May had fallen for a mere captain.

Mrs Goelet's reaction was far worse than May had feared. She disregarded it as nonsense, seeing it as worse than the Duke of Manchester's fiasco, and denied completely and loudly that her daughter could never have even entertained a liaison with a mere army captain!

But May had indeed fallen for the exceedingly handsome – and extremely tall – Captain Oswald Ames of the Royal Lifeguards, the very officer she had seen leading the Jubilee Procession back in 1897.

But the press could not be quashed. They had been

desperate to get a substantial hint of a possible romance for May since 1901, and they waxed lyrical about this 6ft 8in tall gentleman, intrigued because he was a commoner and had no independent income, apart from his captain's salary.

Nevertheless the London office of the *New York Journal & Advertiser* described him as: *'...a magnificent man. He is an ideal Anglo-Saxon. He is a creation of Ouida in real life. His proportions are extremely fine for a man of his height. He is straight and very broad shouldered.'* The article went on to describe the red uniform of the Lifeguards, with its *'shining cuirasses, scarlet coats loaded with gold lace, white breeches and enormous jack boots'*.

Another article described how Captain Ames, aware of his unworthiness of the love of a woman such as May, and not to appear to be a fortune hunter, refrained from declaring his love, but that May, *'with a woman's intuition'*, was aware of his feelings and eager to reciprocate.

At any time this would have been anathema to Mrs Goelet but, as it happened, the timing could not have been worse, for the eager mother had just received a marriage proposal for May from none other than Prince Francis of Teck.

The mere fact that he was a prince was obviously the epitome of all her dreams, because not only would it automatically give May precedence over the Marlboroughs, but Francis was in fact the brother of Mary, the Duchess of York who would one day be the Queen Consort of England. The thought that her daughter could be the sister-in-law of the future queen exceeded all that Mary Goelet had dreamt possible. She could not now believe what had come over her erstwhile so sensible and biddable daughter.

Francis' father, the late Duke of Teck, had married Princess Mary of Cambridge, who was a granddaughter of King William III. But, ironically, despite their social status, the Teck's poverty was legendary. A cruel article published in America when Duchess Mary of Teck died, stated that the *'widower will be obliged to sell or pawn all the silverware and household effects of his late wife in order to pay the butcher, and the baker, and the tailor'*. It was true that but for a small income granted to Mary by the Government after a request by Queen Victoria, the family had nothing. But the Queen had always been particularly fond of their daughter, Mary of Teck, and had chosen her to be engaged to her son Arthur, the then heir to the throne. But, when Arthur died before a marriage had been celebrated, the Queen expressed her wish that after a dignified period Mary should then be engaged to her second son, George, the Duke of York, of whom Mary was very fond and who was the next in line to the throne, securing her future beyond doubt.

But that of her brother Francis held no such promise, hence, an alliance with a fantastically rich American family would have suited Francis extremely well. Moreover, May was beautiful and educated, and would step into a royal role with ease.

But May refused point blank. She was appalled that her mother would consider a man who was a legendary pauper as a husband for her. Besides, he was thirty years old, which was not much older than Captain Ames, as it happened, but Francis lacked the glamour of the latter.

Mrs Goelet was adamant that she would never agree to allow her daughter to marry a mere Army Captain without fortune nor rank – and she still had control over May's inheritance.

After a bitter argument, which May realized she could never win, she finally had no choice but to capitulate. She reluctantly accepted that she must give up all hope of marrying Ames, but she still refused to consider any marriage with Francis and emphatically declared that she would never marry any man whom she did not love.

Mrs Goelet once more realized she must quash her disappointment and, again, adjust her strategy. May had grown up and her mother recognized the emergence of a strength of will in her daughter akin to her own.

Interestingly, the article which so described Captain Ames, also listed, with etched photographs, several of May's other suitors, under the headline: '*MISS MAY GOELET'S DILEMMA – Shall she marry for a title or for love?*' There is a picture of May, and beside the sub-title '*Her mother has picked out a prince, two dukes and an earl for her*', there are images of Francis of Teck, the Duke of Manchester, and Captain Ames, plus a picture of the Duke of Roxburghe, and it says of him: '*Of all the young noblemen who have been mentioned in connection with Miss Goelet, the richest, and in many ways the most dignified, is the Duke of Roxburghe. He was born in 1876, is the eighth duke of his line and is the head of one of the most ancient families in the Scottish Border. He owns 60,000 acres of land and has a splendid place, Floors Castle, in Scotland. His mother was a member of Queen Victoria's household, and a very esteemed friend of the Queen.*

The duchess is a daughter of a previous Duke of Marlborough and an aunt of the present duke who married Miss Consuelo Vanderbilt.

'It is pretty certain that the bride of the Duke of Roxburghe would be received into the very bosom of the royal family. She would have a decided advantage even over the wife of the Duke of Marlborough'.

It is certain that while May kept this article all her life, Kelso would have considered it a great impertinence on behalf of those who wrote and published it. Even though so much of what was said was flattering, he always avoided ambitious mothers and had made no effort to involve himself in the clamour to be May's beau at any time.

Moreover, he saw no reason why the press should discuss what was to him an extremely private matter.

Chapter Five
Gathering Clouds of War

Despite *Society's* endless pursuit of entertainment in these closing years of the nineteenth century, there was growing unease about the situation in South Africa and, as 1899 progressed, war seemed to be inevitable.

Relations with South Africa had been uneasy, even tumultuous on occasion, ever since the end of the Napoleonic Wars earlier in the century.

Both the British and the Dutch Boers had colonized much of South Africa, each with strongly defined, but inevitably opposing opinions on their respective rights.

The British had successfully invaded and occupied the Cape of Good Hope, realizing its invaluable strategic position for controlling all sea routes to The East.

In response to this, the Boers set up their own two Republics in affirmation of what they considered to be *their* territory, namely the Transvaal and the Orange Free State, declaring that Britain was to have no political or legal jurisdiction in either.

This led to heightened tension between the British and Dutch colonials, which was further exacerbated by British frustration when they discovered the practical reality of political impotence when they tried, but failed, to implement anti-slave laws in line with policy back home.

Ironically, the native Zulu and Bantu people were almost totally disregarded in this power struggle throughout the century, and they suffered unspeakably. In fact, the false assumption that British military strength would subjugate the Zulus and pave the way for the development of a linking up of, and strengthening of, British colonies, Dutch republics, and the independent African states. This arrogant plan hoped to group together the above groups under common control, and in 1879 to the greatest military humiliation ever experienced by the British, the Zulu king, Cetshwayo kaMpande, led his army, equipped with shields and spears, against the imperial might of the British Army and wiped out 1300 of their troops and allies.

Inevitably, however, eventually the Zulus were defeated, but not before they had achieved several victories in some notable battles as they held out over a five-month period.

Then, in 1886, gold was discovered in the Transvaal.

Within months, huge numbers of prospectors arrived from Britain, all determined to make their fortunes. They settled and pressed land claims, so that before long the Dutch found themselves outnumbered.

Fearing domination, they started secretly to collect arsenals of the most sophisticated weapons, determined to fight rather than give up what they perceived to be their legitimate position.

The British High Commissioner by 1898 was Alfred Milner, a dedicated servant of the Empire, and his vision was to create a confederation of British colonies throughout Africa, from the Cape to Cairo, for the expansion of trade and for the consolidation of British power.

He also aimed to seize for the Crown the wealth of the goldmines in the Dutch Republics.

Inevitably, his policy destabilized the whole area and a showdown was unavoidable. It began when the Boers launched a surprise offensive in October 1899 and invaded Natal and the Cape Province, which succeeded in them surrounding the three major towns, namely Ladysmith, Mafeking and Kimberley.

War was declared and Britain mustered her troops.

Back in Britain, there was a huge upsurge in patriotism, which called young men to enlist and young women to spur them on to win victory for the Queen. All saw only glory in defending British interests in South Africa, and expected this war to be over in weeks.

At this stage, no-one could see the 1000 days of bloody battling which was to continue until May 1902; and that was to involve 500,000 soldiers from the Empire and Commonwealth, of whom 20,000 died – 1600 of disease or wounds.

No-one could have anticipated the huge loss of Boer lives, either, let alone that this conflict would spawn the infamy of concentration camps - a British invention.

As part of troop mustering, Kelso's Regiment was re-formed in November of that year in preparation for battle. The 1st and 2nd Lifeguards and the Royal Horseguards were amalgamated into the Composite Regiment in 1899, which was created specifically for active service in South Africa.

Kelso and Crichton, as officers in this new Regiment, prepared themselves for imminent dispatch to war.

On the eve of embarkation, Crichton visited May to propose marriage once more, and for him, this time it was serious.

May, loathe to lose his precious friendship by a stark refusal, parried by saying that perhaps she may marry him if he earned a Victoria Cross in action.

Whether or not she, as an American, was aware that it was not possible for one of noble birth to actually win a VC is not clear, but Crichton seemed to accept at last that she would, in fact, never consent to be his bride.

In late November, their Regiment landed in Africa and was deployed to report to General French in time to assist his troops in the relief of the town of Arundel. Troops on the ground were well aware that the arrival of so highly-trained cavalry would not only tremendously boost the morale of French's troops, but it would considerably increase both his command and his mobility.

Hence, when, on December 13th the Boers tried to push south, the British resisted easily, using riflemen on the skirts of the hills and riding the cavalry through the intervening open plains, confidently pushing the enemy back and herded them into the town of Colesberg.

Taking his advantage, and confident that this elite fighting force was about to arrive to support him, French acted decisively and took Rensberg, which had hitherto been the foremost Boer outpost. By now it was December 30th and the reinforcements had not yet arrived, so French found himself stretched to the limit, both holding position and trying to set up a cordon around the enemy.

He maintained position - just.

The Boers, encouraged by an increase of their own manpower, resisted violently. After serious fighting, they managed to re-group, which gave French no option but to stretch his force to the limit in the hope of maintaining the status quo until the promised reinforcements arrived.

Aware of a hiatus, on 4th January, General Shoemann led the Boers in a concerted effort to break through the British cordon with a surprise attack. He succeeded in taking a hill over Colesberg, which gave them a decided advantage as the town lay in a basin surrounded by hills or *kopjes*. A fierce battle ensued, in which the guns of *O Battery* shelled them from the hill and they were pursued by the *10th Hussars* and a squadron of the *Inniskillings (*Inniskilling Fusiliers*)*.

When all seemed desperate, the first of the British reinforcements arrived, led by the Suffolk Regiment, and they ploughed into battle just in time to engage in taking the hill and driving back the Boers.

Kelso and the Composite Regiment were right behind, eager to ride into action under the famed General French.

Indeed they *were* to see action immediately, but serving under Colonel Watson rather than directly under General French. Their assignment was to secure a hill at midnight, under cover of darkness, and reconnoitre Boer positions with the aim of establishing British control.

Kelso, a professional cavalry officer, felt that this was a highly unusual deployment of horse-soldiers. An exercise conducted uphill and in darkness did not allow for the use of horses at all – particularly as silence was crucial for success. Worse than that, the officers were ordered to forfeit their riding boots in favour of canvas shoes for stealth, and to make their men go in stocking feet if they lacked canvas shoes.

From the outset, Kelso had grave misgivings. From what he had seen of the scrubby terrain so far, he had noticed few safe tethering places for a large number of horses, abandoned while their riders went scaling hills in the dark. But he was trained to obey and not to question.

Hence he embarked on the manoeuvre with the others and they crept up the hill, which was much higher than they had anticipated.

Dawn was breaking as they reached the summit and the silence held for a bare minute before there was a volley of shots. Then the air was filled with the raucous clatter and scream of a thousand bullets as they realized they were silhouetted against the morning sky with the guns of the waiting Boers pointing from all three other sides of the hill – and firing mercilessly. They had clambered directly into an ambush.

Watson immediately gave the order to retreat, and at that precise moment he was hit. His body swung round from the impact and he fell – dead.

Instinctively, those who were still alive dropped to the ground and slithered themselves back the way they had come, in a vain attempt to avoid the lethal rain of bullets.

There was no way to discern which Regiment was which, as the survivors gratefully obeyed Watson's dying command to retreat.

But someone in the smoke-filled half-light started to shout commands – and another issued counter commands which made no sense in this insane death trap, so Kelso urged those near him to ignore them and aim for safety and for life. There was no chance that the stocking-footed patrol could fight back against such an attack.

When they reached the foot of the hill, there was total chaos.

Horses, startled by relentless gunfire, had bolted, tearing up their meagre tethering posts. Some soldiers, having scrambled down fastest, had not stopped to look for their own mount but had escaped on the first one they could catch and calm down enough to ride.

Kelso found his own horse, mercifully still where he had left it, and sprang into the saddle with relief. As he turned to ride to safety, he saw one of his own men staggering about, looking for his mount, desperately dodging the bullets that still poured down.

Without hesitation, Kelso turned back, rode into the crossfire and grabbed the man onto his own horse, and together they escaped.

Little was made of this embarrassing incident in the papers back home, although the great Conan Doyle reported the basic facts in his report, *The Great Boer War Ch. IV.* Perhaps Kelso's bravery would also have gone unreported had the young soldier whom he saved not written the account in a letter to his sister in the States. She, in turn, sent the letter to the *New York Herald* and it was published. It read: *'By the time we reached the bottom of the hill, someone had ridden off with my horse so I was left without a mount. The firing was getting rather thick and I thought my last day had come, for I had no chance of getting away on my own.*

'But the Duke of Roxburghe came back for me and I got up on his horse behind him and he carried me safely away from the fire so I owe my life to him'.

Kelso would never have publicized this act of heroism himself, but it was validated and subsequently earned for him the highest award for bravery available to a Scottish nobleman, namely the *Order of the Thistle*. Only sixteen knights and the monarch can hold this honour at any one time, except in rare circumstances. It is not hereditary, and the badge and star of office must be returned to the sovereign after the death of each recipient. It was a tremendous honour, particularly for one as young as Kelso.

Sadly, however, his personal satisfaction in this achievement was diminished by sadness for the loss of so many fellow officers in the campaign. One death in particular that affected him very deeply was that of his own brother-in-law, Major Orr-Ewing, husband of his elder sister, Margaret, and father of her baby daughter. He was killed, bravely attempting to save one of his men.

Kelso's service in South Africa continued through the relief of Kimberley and Paardberg, before the Composite Regiment was recalled to London and then disbanded, and the Royal Blues continued as before in the service of the Queen and the Prince of Wales.

Chapter Six
The Elusive Bride

Having, by this time, well established the ground rules for her future, May continued to enjoy her position as the most eligible heiress on both sides of the Atlantic. And her mother, ever hopeful of the eventual success of her plans, continued to make sure that her daughter was at the heart of Society at the appropriate time, be that in England, France or America. She persisted as the perfect hostess, and treated every potential suitor with impeccable courtesy, no matter how bizarre his case – as she had with Prince Hugo.

In fact, not long after the Hohenlohe affair, there was another German prince who presented himself, unpeturbed by his rival's failure – or perhaps spurred on, thereby.

This was Prince Heinrich Haron of Bavaria, who was also old enough to be May's father. Naturally, he was refused and, no doubt with relief, the Goelets left England for Europe to enjoy the Paris Season.

They entertained sumptuously in the Place Vendome where, before long, Prince Henri of Orleans, the eldest son of the Duc de Chartres and grandson of King Louis Philippe, moved into their circle and eventually presented his offer of marriage.

Henri was 32 years old, tall and good-looking with a

dashing reputation, having once fought a fierce duel with the Count of Turin, nephew of the King of Italy. He was also very different from so many of the other hopefuls, who were mere socialite drifters, for Henri had earned international respect as an explorer, since an expedition as far back as 1889, when he had travelled from Siberia to Siam by way of Tibet. Then after a period in South East Africa in 1892, he journeyed from Hanoi to follow in the footsteps of M.J.F. Garnier, an earlier acclaimed explorer, with the intention of completing his unfinished journey and work on the Mekong River in Indochina (Vietnam).

He went as far as the Brahmaputra, and established the fact that the Thanlwin (Salween) river originates in what was Tibet then, but is now in China. He also discovered the source of the Ayerawady.

His reputation was further enhanced by publishing well accepted accounts of his travels. Two of these were: *Around Tonkin and Siam,* 1894, and *From Tonkin to India* 1897).

The refreshing novelty of this could well have attracted May on an intellectual and romantic level, but, as a woman, she could not overlook the fact, which was well reported, that he had arrived to court her immediately after having been rejected by a beautiful Austrian Princess. Love was certainly not his motivation, therefore, for Miss Goelet, so he was a non-starter.

Sadly, the young man was to die out east in 1901 through a tropical disease, contracted in his travels.

So the Season ended once more with May still mistress of her own heart, much to the intrigued fascination of the press. It was unique, in their experience, that a young lady could have resisted so long against the onslaught of so many eligible noblemen, where others would have capitulated in the dazzle of principalities or dukedoms. But May and her mother went back to Rhode Island again, followed by several European aspirants, and there they were joined also by the American hopefuls.

Four of these equally eligible young men, each reported to be *in love* with the enigmatic and dark-eyed beauty – and, no doubt, her fortune – were Craig Wadsworth, Jimmy Cutting, Jim Woodward – who had long been a *professional* suitor – and, finally, multi-millionaire James Henry Smith.

Gossip columns went so far as to suggest that the youngest of these, possibly Woodward, went so far as to propose to *Mrs* Goelet, on being turned down by her daughter. Naturally, she too refused.

May's complete disinterest in these young men is proven by her failing to bother to keep even one press cutting about them, whereas she did keep many about her aristocratic followers – which also seems to suggest that she was not averse to the idea of marrying into nobility, as her mother wished, provided it was a marriage for love.

Intriguingly, however, there is a letter written by an American suitor later in 1902 which she *did* keep. Sadly, it is unsigned and there was no address, or means of identifying him. He sent it with a cutting from an American newspaper about the fact that the once-so-publicly-spurned Duke of Manchester had travelled to the States, in the hope of trying again for the hand of the lovely May.

In response to this, her hopeful American beau wrote:
'Dear little Lily of Purity,

'On enclosed you will find a clipping from a Chicago morning paper.

'Dear little sweetheart, have nothing to do with these foreign titled beggars. "Little virgin May", if only you knew how debased and un-virtuous that class of men are, you would shrink from them as you would from a reptile. And then, with all your money, you would be to them as one inferior and lower in their estimation. Sweet little May, I hope you will get for a husband a good fine young American like yourself and you may rest assured that joy and happyness (sic) follow. Little Virgin Pet I trust that you will not be angry at the writer for taking this liberty of writing to you. Oh if you were only mine.

'Sincerely yours'.

And perhaps it was this lover, or another equally unrequited, who sent her a newspaper cutting of herself as bridesmaid to her friend, Miss Katherine Duer. He had over-painted May's dress in white, painted a bridal bouquet in her hand, and, at her feet, he added a collage of a winged cupid reaching up to her out of a broken but fiercely burning heart, resting on a lyre set on a cushion. Beside it, he painted another dark-red cushion with a ducal coronet thereon, looking cold and impersonal.

Beneath this he wrote: '*Preference of eternal and disinterested love for the merits Of your angelic sympathy (sic) and the sublimity of your soul* (sic)'.

But, once again, May remained mistress of her own heart, and, although she kept these tokens, she made no mark on them either, to identify their sender(s), nor to hint at whether they pleased, displeased or merely amused her.

Chapter Seven
Tour on the Royal Yacht Ophir

While suitors performed their ritual pirouetting around May, things for Kelso were about to take a dramatic change.

In January 1901, Queen Victoria died at last and the Prince of Wales became King Edward VII.

The gloomy, perennial mourning of Victoria's court ended as the new king refreshed, modernized and refurbished the long-neglected Buckingham Palace, and held glittering evening courts there.

Events planned before the queen's death had to be rescheduled, as the heir took up his responsibilities. Probably the most outstanding of these was the proposed visit to Australia and the Commonwealth. The previous September, Parliament had passed a bill, which had been ratified by Royal Proclamation declaring that '*on and after January 1st 1901, the people of New South Wales, Victoria, South Australia, Queensland, Tasmania and Western Australia should be united in a Federal Commonwealth under the name of the Commonwealth of Australia*'. To mark the occasion it had been planned that the Prince of Wales should travel to Australia to represent the Crown and thereafter tour the whole Commonwealth.

On his accession to the throne, this became impossible.

Not only had the coronation not yet taken place, but it would be out of the question for a new monarch to be out of the country for the proposed seven months of the tour. It was decided, therefore, that Prince George, Duke of York, Edward's son and now heir to the throne, should represent him instead, with his wife, Princess Mary.

This was, moreover, an invaluable opportunity to confirm, by sending the prince in his new role, the importance the new king placed in his relations with the Commonwealth.

Kelso, now 25, was chosen by the king to serve the Duke of York in the Royal Suite as Aide de Campe, and he prepared himself for a journey which was to take from 15th March to 31st October that year. It was the longest period he was to be away from Britain in his whole life, and he was to visit all of the countries of the Commonwealth.

Of the other officers chosen to serve Prince George, there were three of his closest friends, Lord Crichton, Prince Alexander of Teck – another brother of Princess Mary – and Commander Geoffrey Fausset, and they were joined by Colonel Byron of the Australian Artillery and Major Bor of the Marines.

The Head of Household, or Chief of Staff, was Lord Wenlock, a man highly respected by the king, who had elevated him to the Privy Council only days before departure. Privy Secretary to the prince was Sir Arthur Bigge, who had worked his way up from groom-in-waiting to the rank of Private Secretary to the late queen. The king chose to send Bigge, confident that he would be a wise advisor to the prince, a niche he was to fill until he died in 1931, by which time he was a much valued friend to George also.

The assistant Private Secretary was Sir Donald Mackenzie Wallace, from the Colonial Office, and the prince's Equerry was the Honourable Derek Keppel, who was brother-in-law to Mrs George Keppel, long-term mistress of the king.

Mrs Derek Keppel was a companion to Princess Mary, but she was also chosen because she had previously had beneficial diplomatic links with Australia, due to the fact that her sister, Lady Carrington, had lived there when her husband was Governor of New South Wales in 1888.

Moreover, as she, like the princess, had had to leave her very young family in the care of nannies and family, they had much in common, and would be moral support to each other.

Finally, there were two artists in the Suite, one of whom, Chevalier de Martino, had been marine artist to the late queen.

The Ladies in Waiting to the duchess were Lady Mary Lygon and Lady Katherine Cook – pronounced Coke. The Domestic Chaplain was Canon Dalton, and the Medical Attendant was Dr Manby.

So, on 15th March, Kelso joined the rest of the Suite on the special train that had been laid on at Victoria Station to take them to Portsmouth.

There they went on board the almost new steamship, the *Ophir,* which had been upgraded to the status of a Royal yacht specifically for the tour because the existing yacht, the *Victoria and Albert*, was an aged paddle steamer and in no way fit for such a journey.

Although the royal apartments on board were sumptuous, Kelso was unimpressed with the cabin he was to share with Crichton, and described it as a *'regular dog box'*.

Nevertheless, he unpacked his things and was ready for

5pm when King Edward and Queen Alexandra came on board for tea. Afterwards, they inspected the whole ship, including Kelso's cabin. Later, he went onshore for a farewell dinner at Admiralty House, with his mother and sister, Via, who were staying there to see him off.

The following morning, there was a huge parade, at which the sailors – or Bluejackets – were presented with their South African medals from the king, after which the Royal couple came on board to join their son and his wife at a final formal luncheon before they sailed.

At 3.45p.m. an emotional Edward and Alexandra took their leave, and the *Ophir* sailed at precisely 4 o'clock, preceded by the old Royal Yacht, bearing the King and Queen, and escorted by destroyers, to a blaze of salutes from the onshore forts.

Lady Anne and Via watched from the Admiral's barge, which was among the flotilla of other boats assembled to wish them bon voyage.

Once they reached the river bar, the *Victoria and Albert* turned back and the *Ophir* sailed on, escorted by the *Diadem* and the *Niobe*.

That evening, Kelso enjoyed a quiet dinner on board, at which the duchess did not appear, as she was overtired.

Kelso was both embarrassed and irritated with himself that he took several days to find his sea legs. He mentioned in his diary that on 18t^h March, 'he *dined in the ward room but had to leave hurriedly about 10, owing to the motion aft. Relieved to find others in our saloon, 'hors de combat'.*

He always refers to seasickness in these terms or some other euphemistic way, and seemed to take little comfort in the fact that Prince George was dogged with this infliction all his life, even though he had been in the Navy and actually going to sea since he was thirteen years old. Several times throughout the voyage, however, he does make tactful entries such as, '*HRH did not appear on deck today. Slight swell*'.

The first port of call was Gibraltar, and procedures there set the pattern for what was to happen throughout the tour. At the official landing, there was always a procession through the eager crowds, followed by a medal celebration, in which the duke decorated those who had served in the Boer War.

The organisation or over-viewing of these presentations was one of Kelso's specific responsibilities, together with one of the other ADCs, and perfection was always his target. Should anything, particularly the incompetence of authorities on shore disrupt the smooth running of any ceremonial, he was extremely irritated because he felt it inconvenienced the prince.

Once the formalities were over, there were lunches and patriotic displays or dinners, followed by concerts which frequently culminated in fireworks and illuminated displays, both on land and on the flotillas of crafts, large and small, which gathered in every harbour to greet them.

On arrival at each destination, Kelso's major concern was the quality of horses provided for himself and his fellow officers. Being the owner of a fine stable, and having served in the Royal Blues for his whole adult life, he was accustomed to riding only the best. He was ever aware of the importance of the dignity which should at all times attend every royal procession, and that any mount provided to ride escort between rows of cheering, excited people should be reliable.

As it happened, Gibraltar challenged his skill in horsemanship to the limit, by providing for him what Kelso described as '*a weird dark bay pony which I quite dwarfed*'. The image becomes more vivid if one recalls the length of his legs in thigh-length jack boots, which must have been folded almost double in the stirrups.

Naturally, the dignitaries in each port were eager to take the Royal Party to visit their major sights, and Kelso was able to enjoy this either in attendance on the Yorks when on duty, or as one of the party of important guests when not.

Whenever possible, if there was time, he also liked to explore the shops or other local attractions, alone or with a friend. But duties were heavy – if enjoyable. Usually, whenever there had been a banquet on shore, for example, there was a return banquet on board the *Ophir*. When they were in Gibraltar, it was held on the last evening, on a day otherwise marred by murky weather. But, to Kelso's delight, as the meal finished, they went on deck to find it had cleared up entirely, just in time for the most spectacular display of fireworks and illuminations.

The following morning, they set course for Malta, through the Mediterranean, off Algiers. Communication through Marconi radio was still novel, and Kelso was intrigued when *Diana*, one of their escort ships, linked by radio to Malta through chains of boats posted alongside the African coast.

Their subsequent arrival at Malta was suitably spectacular. A fleet of ten destroyers met the *Ophir* about ten miles offshore, and manoeuvred round them at high speed, firing salutes and then preceded them into the harbour, which was full of warships; the quayside was lined with massed troops and welcoming crowds.

Of course, by this time, Prince George had already achieved the rank of Commander in the Navy in his own right, and so the display was to honour him both in this rank and as heir to the throne and representative of his father. To Kelso, the perfect discipline of this spectacular welcome, together with its appropriateness in acknowledging the prince's service rank were deeply satisfying.

Once they had landed, they repeated the formula established in Gibraltar, but, for Kelso, the highlight of his visit was the chance to play a game of polo. He found the hard ground heavy going and once again complained of the shortness of the horses, but he didn't let these minor problems detract from the enjoyment of the sport.

Later, after the medal-giving, and having escorted the prince on his official visit to the Naval hospital, Kelso really enjoyed driving with the duchess, informally, to visit the Chapel of Bones, which intrigued him. It had been built in 1612 by the Order of the Hospitallers of St John, alongside their hospital, the Sacra Infermeria, and the walls of the chapel were lined with skeletons, skulls and bones. It was to be destroyed by bombs in WW II.

After this, they went to the governor's country palace, where he was enchanted by the gardens, which were full of ripened orange trees, roses, freesias and creepers.

In each destination, Kelso was minutely interested in the land and its produce, which he loved to compare or contrast with those of his own vast estates in the Scottish Border lands.

The fireworks display that night Kelso described as unforgettable, because each warship had rigged up lights to transform themselves into the shapes of prehistoric creatures, which were then towed between the vessels in the harbour. By the time they set sail at midnight, Kelso was exhausted and relished the prospect of the three days ahead to be spent at sea en route for Port Said and the Suez Canal.

They arrived there at about 3pm on 30th March, but Kelso failed to be impressed, describing it as *'dirty and smelly'*.

They hosted Lord Cromer, the Governor of Port Said and the Khedive's brother on board for an official dinner, after which the crew and a large number of Arabs worked until 4am *coaling*, or loading the huge amounts of coal on board that were essential for the long journey ahead. The unrelenting noise, the heat and the dust all combined to give Kelso a thoroughly bad night.

Progress through the Suez Canal next day was slow, hampered by the fact that the *Brittanic* had run aground in the canal, and by nightfall this was compounded by news that one of the dredgers had broken down, too. It was then decided that it would be unsafe to try to squeeze past in the dark, so the decision was taken to drop anchor and wait until daylight. But by Tuesday, April 2nd they had safely reached the Red Sea and the weather was hot and pleasant. Kelso chose to sleep on deck. The heat increased as they approached Aden, and the sea was so calm Kelso described it as a *mill pond*. A passing P&O liner on its way back home triggered a pang of homesickness, and prompted Kelso to write letters so that they could be posted in Aden.

They spent only three days in Aden, and Kelso found the heat oppressive. He was really relieved to escape from the formal reception fairly early that night to enjoy the cooler evening air.

As they sailed on into the Indian Ocean, the heat and humidity increased. To entertain them on one of the long evenings at sea, the crew presented a concert, wearing costumes, some hired in London before they left and some intriguingly made up from items found on board. Diverting as this was, Kelso didn't adapt well to the heat which he described as '*beastly hot and muggy*', and he still seemed to be hankering for home when, once again, he spots a '*big liner homeward bound*'.

Their next destination was Columbo in Ceylon – now Sri Lanka – and Kelso was wakened by the sound of the salute being fired as they entered the harbour. As always, there were many vessels there to welcome them, among which he noticed one that was carrying Boer prisoners of war.

Although he found the national dress of the Celonese natives '*very weird*', he was surprised and much impressed at the quality and comfort of the train which they boarded to make a journey inland to a town called Kandy, through dense, tropical vegetation which reminded Kelso of parts of Africa in its lush beauty.

Kelso was far more comfortable in Kandy, as it was 1600 feet above sea level and was considerably cooler and fresher.

He and Crichton were billeted in a bungalow '*made of palm leaves*', which in itself was cooler but, should they feel the heat, there were natives standing by to fan them with the punkahs.

At 6.30 the following morning, Kelso borrowed a pony and enjoyed a '*glorious ride*' before breakfast. Then some native traders were allowed in to display their wares on a billiard table and Kelso joined the others in haggling over prices as he added to his growing collection of souvenirs. Although he did try bartering, he felt later that he should have persevered longer, admitting ruefully in the diary '*I suppose I was done*'.

Before lunch, colours and medals were presented to the Ceylon Mounted Infantry, which was followed by a native entertainment for the Suite which, extraordinarily, included the parading of some '*absolutely wild bushmen who had been specially caught for the occasion*'. Kelso is astounded that they '*did not know the value of money*'.

On the Sunday after his dawn ride, Kelso had to present himself to Church at 11.30 am in full frock uniform, including helmet, and he found it '*beastly hot*'. But later in the day, he really appreciated a visit to the Botanical Gardens, after which they went to watch a parade of elephants which bathed in the river for their amusement. The elephants were then made to display their strength by pushing down fair-sized trees.

Two days later, the young duke left Columbo, having done more shopping, attended more functions and having written more letters home because *Pomone,* one of their escort ships, had completed her tour of duty and was turning homeward. The *Ophir,* however, proceeded towards Singapore where, although still irked by the heat, Kelso enjoyed travelling in *gharries*, or small sedan carts drawn by Burmese ponies, and he loved the pretty Chinese lanterns decorating the streets.

Just before leaving, Kelso again managed a game of polo, and although he found the horse acceptable this time, he criticized the saddlery as '*old and vile*'. He and Crichton went back on board ahead of the rest to organize the big farewell luncheon before sailing.

Once back at sea, they passed various vessels, all of which saluted the Duke and Duchess of York, and Kelso noticed the incongruity of two Japanese warships as they passed.

It was at this point that they actually crossed the Equator and the prince had agreed to allowing the time-honoured traditional festivities for *crossing the line*. However, the death of a stoker on board had delayed the celebration for a day or so while they organized the funeral at sea.

Once the formalities were over, everyone threw themselves into the enjoyment of the experience, particularly those, like Kelso, who had never experienced it before.

On the eve of the chosen day, a *'terrible voice'* seemed to boom from below *Ophir's* bow. It challenged the captain on behalf of Neptune, god of the sea, to declare what ship this was, who travelled aboard and what was their destination. The officer on watch answered that the ship belonged to King Edward, and was carrying the Duke and Duchess of York to Australia. The voice then welcomed the Royal couple in his master's name, and promised that the very next day *'Neptune himself would grace the deck with his presence'*.

Early next day, the Thursday, the crew set up a large canvas tank filled with water, in which 'Neptune's' *victims* would be 'baptised'. Then, at about 10am, an incredible chariot appeared, apparently made of seashells and carrying 'Neptune', with three figures to represent Britannia, Australia and Canada. It was drawn by a guard of honour, made up of the biggest Marines on board, all dressed in outlandish costumes. They presented those in the chariot to their Royal

Highnesses. Then 'Neptune' stepped down and sprinkled water over the head of the duchess, declaring her the *Queen of the Seas*. Then his 'wife' presented her with a beautiful bouquet of coral. 'Neptune', meanwhile, continued to 'baptise' the other ladies.

But for the men it was far more ruthless. A chair was erected precariously near the edge of the bath where 'Neptune's' barber waited for his victims.

Beginning with the prince, each man was shaved – or half shaved – then tipped into the bath for a severe ducking by the waiting 'sea-bears'. Should anyone open his mouth to protest, it was filled with lather. It is worth noticing that although each participant was 'shaved', neither the prince nor any of his Suite lost their fine moustaches – not even half a moustache, according to official photographs taken soon afterwards – but lesser ranks were not so fortunate.

Kelso was uncomfortable with such boisterous behaviour, but was obviously sporting enough to join in. In fact, he claimed to have robbed '*Neptune, the stud groom*' of his beard before they managed to fling him in.

But the young duke was to suffer for the escapade. To start with, the sea was becoming very choppy during the festivities, to the point where the ducking tank was violently churned up. Then one of the men tried to resist the barber by hurling himself at one of the biggest of the 'barbers', knocking him into the pool, followed immediately by six Bluejackets, swearing revenge. The sides of the tank gave way, spewing water and men everywhere.

By this time, Neptune had vanished – as probably had the Yorks and their immediate retinue that is the ladies and the more mature gentlemen. But the revelries carried on in the ward rooms long into the night once the men were dried and changed. The next day Kelso was very unwell with severe earache, which he blamed on his ducking. Many of the men were unwell, in fact, suffering from both seasickness and hangovers.

Even though the doctor saw Kelso on the second night, he was little improved and his discomfort continued to be compounded by the heavy swell as the boat ran into the North-East trade winds. Most of the party were levelled by this and, amongst others, the duchess did not appear on deck all that day.

But, by Sunday, after a good night's sleep, Kelso woke to find the sea dead calm with only the slightest swell, and he was recovered enough to attend the church service with the others – including the duchess.

Now they were sailing south, down the western coast of Australia past Perth, and the weather, to Kelso's relief, was becoming cooler.

Ophir negotiated Cape Leeuwin to berth in Albany, at the southernmost tip of Australia. They docked for barely twenty-four hours, but Kelso took the opportunity to write letters to catch the mail before they moved on.

During the following days at sea, heading for Melbourne, deck sports were organized. Kelso and his partner 'Gropy' Fausset won the wheelbarrow race. He also really enjoyed a game of deck cricket. But he was longing to land, particularly as he was expecting to meet up with some special, long-time friends, among who were Lord and Lady Hopetoun, the State Governor and his wife, whom Kelso always affectionately called Lord & Lady Hopey. Another old family friend and fellow officer, Duffy, was to be there, and they had much to catch up on.

For Kelso, it was to be a welcome link with home. One day in the future, relations between the two men were to become strained when Duffy wanted to marry one of Kelso's sisters and, as he had no fortune, Lady Anne, Kelso's mother, strongly opposed the match, giving Kelso no choice but to agree. But, at this period, their friendship was intact and their reunion was genuinely anticipated.

Always meticulous and observant of protocol himself, Kelso found the exuberant informality of the Australian crowd hard to accept, but some of the unusual entertainments like the display of riding on bucking wild horses he really enjoyed.

The days leading up to the opening of the Federal Parliament on May 9th were a constant round of functions for the Yorks and their Suite, each of which Kelso suffered, tolerated or enjoyed. The actual opening of the Parliament, however, with all the dignified pomp and ceremony with the heir present in the name of the king, he really enjoyed because it was staged faultlessly.

The news reporters of the time commented on the lack of colour in the clothing of the huge throng of dignitaries who were official guests at the ceremony, because all the ladies wore the mourning shades of blacks, grey and mauves because of the recent death of the late queen. Hence, people rejoiced in the rich colours of the officers in their ceremonial uniforms which added a welcome relief from the monotony.

Satisfied as Kelso had been in the ceremonial of the earlier part of the day, he was appalled at the inefficiency in the procedural protocol for the evening reception. The Australians were inexperienced in stage managing a social function on this scale and in the presence of Royalty, so the ensuing chaos was deeply irritating to Kelso.

For a start, there was minimal communication between the police and the military security who were trying to filter invited guests into Government House before the arrival of the prince, and little planning had been given to managing such numbers of carriages converging at the same time through the same gateway to the one house entrance.

Hence, there was a huge hold-up and, knowing the Duke of York's obsession with punctuality, those riding ahead were agitated by the inability to create a clear passage for him.

Miraculously, in the event, all was smoothed out by the time he actually did arrive, and everyone was in place when the fanfare sounded and they all stood for the National Anthem.

Then the royal party was escorted to a flower-decked dais which was cordoned off, but it had been placed in such a position that once the room was full, barely anybody could see the prince or princess, particularly as George was so short.

It was Prince George himself who immediately noticed the unrest as people strained to see him, and he resolved the situation by directing the governor, Lord Hopetoun, to lead the party up and down the room so that everyone could comfortably view their royal guests.

A newspaper later reported that as they processed, bowing to the delighted guests, '*Two immense guardsmen, the Duke of Roxburghe and Viscount Crichton, equerries to His Royal Highness... making a path through the people who were packed too tightly'.*

The following day, Kelso was on duty in drizzling rain at a military review, which he thought was a good performance, particularly the display given by 4,000 cadets, but after lunch he had to endure a concert, which he described as an '*awful performance.* Maybe his opinion was coloured by the fact that he had to stand throughout in full uniform.

But on the Monday, they were given leave and Kelso, Crichton and a few friends headed out of Melbourne for a whole day's shooting. The following day, after escorting the prince to the Exhibition Buildings, they were again free, this time to take the overnight train with the prince to Chilmany Park for another shoot.

Kelso was well satisfied with that day's bag which he listed as follows:

132 brace of quail;

10 parrots (which Kelso described as beautiful birds!)

3 hares;

1 snake – shot by HRH.

Having had a thoroughly enjoyable day, it was rounded off to perfection for Kelso when he learned that the next part of the schedule, a visit to Brisbane, had been curtailed because of an outbreak of plague there and Kelso was granted permission to arrange a trip up the country for himself, Cust and Faussett.

For seven glorious days, Kelso devoted himself to his favourite pastimes – riding and shooting. He shot stags, hares, cockatoos, kangaroo rats; in fact, anything that moved. He enjoyed the company of his hosts, Lord and Lady Curzon, and their house-guests but, most of all, he revelled in the fresh air and the freedom. Moreover, by now the temperature was dropping, particularly at night, and as he was healthily exhausted after each day's exertions, he had no difficulty sleeping.

At last, however, he had to catch the horse-drawn bus with the others at 5.30 am on the Saturday, to be taken to the train station to return to their duties.

Their journey through New South Wales was pleasantly comfortable and very picturesque. When they finally arrived in Sydney at 4.45pm, Kelso was pleased to meet up with the others, and they all went back on board at 9pm at Hawkesbury River, where *Ophir* was moored.

That Sunday, May 26th was the Princess Mary's birthday, and Kelso was proud that the gift from himself and the other ADCs had been his choice, a silver Kangaroo, and it had been graciously received. The day was celebrated with a picnic up the river, at a site they reached in a paddle steamer, which made a pleasant change. Kelso thought the scenery fine but a little boring, or as he put it '*too much sameness*'.

Once back on board, Kelso caught up with his letter writing so as to catch the next mail.

The following week, *Ophir* left the Hawkesbury River and as they reached the Heads outside Sydney Harbour, they were met by the Australian Squadron, and various other boats, and the tour recommenced.

Kelso was pleased that the weather was fine, as it helped to make their departure so attractive, with all the colourful escort. He was always aware of what impression they made on those watching onshore and in the waters around them, surprisingly so for such a private man.

The next week was full of the familiar rounds of duties, dinners, concerts and medal ceremonies, all of which Kelso observed with a professional eye, but he was relieved when, on June 3rd, which was the prince's birthday, they had just one tedious engagement, then went to a steeplechase at Raudwick Racecourse, and then on to the station to take a trip up country for another shooting party and, although the spoils were poor, Kelso loved the freedom and the good riding.

On returning to Sydney, they boarded the *Ophir* and, with the usual ceremonies, set course for New Zealand. Kelso was saddened to be leaving his dear friends, the Hopetouns, and his spirits were further lowered because the sea was decidedly choppy, and many were laid low with seasickness.

To make matters even worse for him, it was time for him to take his turn to make up the on-board bridge accounts, which was the one task he hated above all others.

On June 10th they anchored in Auckland Harbour. Immediately, Kelso was captivated by how pretty the place was, so full of trees and so green. When the rain stopped and he went for a walk he was delighted to see hedges and even gorse. That night he wrote, somewhat poignantly in his diary, *'in fact, one might be in England' (or Scotland?)*.

The next day, they began the familiar round of duties, but this particular opening ceremony was to stay in Kelso's mind, because of an accident in the procession.

He was fortunate to have been given a quiet horse, which was apparently better than Crichton's. But, as they processed towards a huge, heavily-festooned archway on Queen's Wharf, one of the horses leading the second carriage immediately behind the prince's, slipped and fell. Fortunately, no-one was hurt and the occupants were swiftly transferred to another carriage, but, from then on, Kelso was on edge for the safety of the Royal couple, particularly as there were frequent blockages along the way as enthusiastic crowds spilled into their path.

Kelso really loved the places they visited in New Zealand, particularly when they travelled by special train to Rotorura where they saw the geysers and mud springs in Whokarewera and Tikative. And everywhere they went, the Maoris sang and danced for them, and heaped them with gifts of rugs, feather mats, meris – Maori war clubs, 12-18 inches long made of hardwood, whalebone or greenstone which was a local variety of jade – and other things, most of which had great tribal significance.

From Auckland they travelled to Wellington, from where they took the train inland to Christchurch and Dunedin. Everywhere there were the ceremonies and banquets, and in each place Kelso relished the opportunity to spend time in the countryside, with its arable land fenced in with bright gorse hedges, because it so much reminded him of his own beautiful estates back home. He was even delighted to see Border Leicesters and Cheviots, breeds of sheep native to his own Scottish Border countryside, and was intrigued to learn that they were bred because of their suitability for the frozen meat trade.

At the end of June, they set sail for Tasmania, then on to Hobart, enduring more rough seas on the way. From there, they progressed to Adelaide, where the seas were so rough the party had to be landed by tug. There, Kelso had four day's leave and he headed back to Melbourne by train where, in addition to riding and hunting, he spent two days at the Flemington Racecourse, where he also attended the Flemington Grand National. While there, he regretted not acting on a tip to back a horse called 'Lucidon', because it did come in first.

On arriving back in Adelaide, he was surprised that the prince had sent a comfortable car to meet himself and his friends at the station.

Once back on board, they were forced to push through heavy seas which once more laid low many of the Royal party, so the prince decided to turn back to Albany to take a train to Perth instead. This unexpectedly afforded time for Kelso to ride for pleasure between duties, but he sounded really homesick when, on 25th July, he wrote that it was the first time he'd spent his birthday away from home.

The following day, they left Australasia, waved off by a huge crowd. The *Ophir* was the first Royal Yacht to have its own band which, on this occasion, made their departure very emotional. Lined up on deck, they played some old familiar and patriotic songs from Britain, obviously starting with *God Save the King*. *Auld Lang Syne* was followed by *Rule Britannia*, and everyone onshore sang along lustily. The finale, however, was *Home Sweet Home* and, at this, the crowd fell poignantly silent.

After a pause, Prince George broke the tension by stepping forward and shouting loudly, '*Three Cheers for Australia*'. The crew responded enthusiastically and the crowd erupted in ecstatic delight. The *Ophir* slipped away and set sail for Mauritius before heading for Durban.

This part of the voyage was, once again, beset by strong winds, and as they approached harbour in Durban the seas were so high that it was necessary to transport the Suite in small groups by basket into the waiting tender. The basket was like a tall, oval wicker-work lift cubicle with an open doorway, and it was winched across from the ship to the boat.

When it was Kelso's turn, he travelled with Mr & Mrs Keppel and Lady Katherine Coke. He did not enjoy the experience and later expressed gratitude that it was the only time throughout the tour that they were forced to resort to this form of conveyance. What he did not record, perhaps because he was blissfully unaware of it at the time, was that below them there were sharks circling. However, a petty officer named Harry Price happened to be on duty at the time described the scene in gleeful detail and painted a delightful little watercolour of it in his own diary.

At this time, the Boer War was still rumbling on and there had been much debate in Parliament as to whether it was safe for George, the heir apparent, to risk landing in Durban, South Africa.

Mr Chamberlain, the Prime Minister, felt that not allowing the visit would give the Boers a great propaganda coup, so he urged it to go ahead.

George, himself, had absolutely no doubt in his mind. Having wanted to serve in the war from the outset, and having spent almost five months awarding medals across the world to those who *had* fought for the Crown in this war, he was adamant that as heir to the throne he should definitely put in an appearance to raise the morale of those still fighting.

So it went ahead and was a huge success. Lord Kitchener came down to meet the prince so that he could personally deliver a progress report.

Kelso, who was obviously keenly interested in the campaign in which he had served with such bravery, was highly honoured that George sent for him that evening and gave him a confidential update of the situation.

When they arrived at Capetown, the British settlers greeted the Royal couple with wild and patriotic enthusiasm.

While there, Kelso wanted to have the opportunity to see at close quarters one of the concentration camps set up to hold Boer prisoners of war; men, women and children. They had already glimpsed the site from deck as the ship entered harbour.

The Colonel in Chief readily gave him permission, and a small group of officers was able to visit and view the prisoners through wire enclosures.

Kelso's report, reticent as ever, even in his private diary was simple and without any personal comment or opinion.

Finally, on August 3rd they embarked for Canada and for twelve days were sailing with little to report, except the change in escort ships.

On September 13th, the eve of their arrival, they heard of the attempted assassination of the American President, McKinley. In fact, by the time they actually arrived, the battle to save McKinley had been lost and President Theodore Roosevelt had been sworn in.

Dense fog greeted their arrival at the St Lawrence River, and prevented the prince from meeting the Governor General as planned, so the official landing was postponed until 12.30p.m. the following day.

On this occasion, Kelso was unimpressed by his horse, the rainy weather, and the *'rotten review'* they were subjected to.

To him the only redeeming feature of the day was the medal ceremony which is fairly certain he himself had stage-managed.

To make matters worse, he was thoroughly depressed at the prospect of travelling to Montreal by train, having heard that the train had no baths and no individual rooms.

In fact, the train was not nearly as bad as reported, which was fortunate as they spent a considerable amount of time on it throughout the Canadian leg of the tour. Kelso adapted to the new routines, one of which was to stop for a full hour each morning to allow the Duchess of York to dress in comfort.

In Ottawa, for the unveiling of an official statue, Kelso was appalled to learn that the local general had given his men permission not to appear in khaki uniform for the occasion. To Kelso's relief, this had been overruled by the Ministry.

Throughout the tour, Kelso's criticism of weaknesses in military performance at any level had become more overt, and caused him real irritation. Nevertheless, it was not sufficient to mar his enjoyment of every other aspect of the trip, particularly if it included the chance to ride, hunt or participate in any sporting activity, even by observation.

He keenly observed the agricultural variations in the territories through which they travelled, comparing methods of farming and management with his own land back home. He was fascinated to see the vast timber works and the logging demonstrations laid on for them, and was interested in the types of pine trees grown and harvested. Moreover, he loved the majestic scenery – although he preferred the snow to stay on the distant mountains!

In late September, after a brief visit to Vancouver Island,

they returned to the mainland to take the train across the Rockies to Banff. The scenery was so breathtaking, Kelso often chose to travel on what he called the *cowcatcher*, out in front of the train, which afforded the passengers an uninterrupted view of the whole panorama.

On arrival, the ladies were comfortably ensconced in a hotel for a rest. Kelso, the prince and nine other men set off for a shooting expedition at Prairie, Manitoba, near Prairie Point. They were met at the station by a Canadian senator, John Nesbitt Kirchoffer, and they travelled in horse-drawn carriages towards the Delta Marsh along the banks of Lake Manitoba. Then they transferred to canoes for the final five miles to Kirchoffer's cabin, where they had two glorious days' shooting.

To Kelso's delight, when they arrived back to rejoin the others at the hotel, the prince sent Kelso and Keppel for a further couple of hours sport. They obeyed with alacrity and were picked up later that day.

Much refreshed, the party resumed their journey on a very juddering train to Toronto for more public engagements, before moving on to visit Lake Niagara.

Kelso's first sight of the rapids was from the opposite side below Brock's Monument, where he took the electric train up to a vantage point, still on the Canadian side, overlooking the gorge. He was much impressed with this *'wonderful sight'*, after which he scrambled down the cliffs to view the *'rush of water near to where Captain Webb was last seen'*, after his failed attempt to swim these treacherous rapids.

The Captain Webb Kelso had referred to in his diary was the first English man known to have swum the English

Channel, in 1875, at the age of twenty-seven. Years later, he took his family to the Niagara Falls in a vain attempt to rekindle his faded glory by trying to swim a particularly treacherous part of the Niagara River. Against advice, he dived into the '*lethal rapids and whirlpool*', swam well at first, then hit the whirlpool and was seen no more until his body was dragged from the river, downstream, five days later.

Kelso's party proceeded past a couple of suspension bridges, passing the American and Horseshoe Falls, and he was much impressed by 'the *wonderful rush of water*'. After this, they were driven round Goab Island, getting out for a period on both the Canadian and American sides, finishing up on the latter, where Kelso joined the rest of the party to take a tram to Lewiston, where they caught a boat back to the *Ophir*.

While the Royal suite had been onshore, travelling round Canada, the crew of *Ophir* had completely scrubbed the boat down, scraped off all rust, and given her a fresh coat of paint so that she looked as new as when they had left Portsmouth over six months before.

Now they had only one other destination before setting course back home and that was to Newfoundland, which they approached in a swirling snowstorm.

By now, Kelso was longing for home and eagerly counting the hours. His diary petered out at this stage, except for minimal weather reports as they crossed the Atlantic. Then, on October 30th, he was delighted to see the Channel Fleet of six battleships and nine cruisers, steaming out to escort them in, and was so excited as they manoeuvred, firing the salute. His joy was complete when, that evening at dinner, George personally thanked all his staff for making the Commonwealth

Tour an absolute success.

The journey had taken Kelso 45,000 miles, 33,032 of which had been by sea. The Duke of York had laid 21 foundation stones; received 544 addresses; presented 4,329 medals and had shaken hands with 24,855 people at official receptions alone, and Kelso had been beside him as ADC at a considerable number of these occasions. But he was delighted to be back in Britain, and couldn't wait to return to his family and his beautiful home in Scotland. [1]

---

[1] Statistics from Prince George's personal diary 1901. Kelso's Diary: A Duke's Diary edited & Annotated by Rosaleen Moorhead Murphy. Published 2004 Craigholme Publishers

Chapter 8
A Surfeit of Suitors

By 1902, May had still not chosen her future husband and the Press continued to watch her every move and to read romance into each encounter, and, inevitably, through that year there were a couple that attracted particular attention.

The first was Viscount Ingestre, whom May had met on several occasions when visiting the Pembrokes at Wilton. As mentioned previously, May felt at home with the Pembrokes, and treated their son, Lord Herbert, more as a brother than a potential husband, and she felt quite relaxed in the company of his close friends.

Hence, when Viscount Ingestre joined them in Wilton again that summer, May, for once, underestimated the level of Press vigilance, and did nothing to prevent them observing the easy friendship she shared with him.

Viscount Ingestre was young, handsome and was the heir of the Earl of Shrewsbury and Talbot, Premier Earl of the Realm who, therefore, outranked all his peers. One cannot help but feel that Mrs Goelet watched May's obvious pleasure in this young man's company with anticipation and some prayer that, at last, her daughter may be falling in love appropriately... because, for once, it was not about money.

Indeed, May was able to enjoy his company, aware that

there was no such hidden agenda because, in his own right, he stood to inherit vast wealth in addition to the ancestral estates, because his father had increased his fortunes in the way that would have been so much admired by her own late father. The earl was the owner of the Brereton Collieries, in themselves highly lucrative in the early years of the nineteenth century, but, in addition, he owned the leading cab firm in London. He was, in other words, a highly successful business entrepreneur.

Ingestre was heir to all of this and, in addition, he was a also a dashing young officer in the Royal Horseguards – besides being excellent company. Moreover, his family had a colourful past which the American Press enjoyed exploiting with relish.

Twenty five years earlier, his father, the earl, had shocked society by eloping with a divorcee, with much theatrical drama involving trains and yachts. There were tales of duels over the affair, and the countess' mother attacked the earl with her umbrella at the railway station when the two eventually returned.

Then the Bishop of Chester forbade any of his clergy to give the couple Communion. Nevertheless, public sympathy was with them and by the time of Edward's eventual coronation (which had been delayed because he had appendicitis on the eve of the original date), the countess was allowed to take her place at the head of the peeresses at the ceremony.

Much as May enjoyed this interlude, there was no engagement, despite the bitter disappointment – again – of her mother and the bewilderment of the Press. But, as always, there was another suitor waiting in the wings who followed

May back to Newport, and this was Grand Duke Boris of Russia.

Boris was a cousin of the Tsar and, at the time, was heir presumptive to the Russian throne, as Nikolai so far had only produced daughters, who, by Russian law, were not eligible to succeed. It was rumoured that when news of his pursuit of May reached St Petersburg, Boris had had a summons to return there forthwith but, it seemed, Boris was prepared even to forfeit his right to the throne if May would agree to marry him.

May was by now twenty-three, and this was the sixteenth nobleman to seriously pay her court. She was amused by the heavy, flamboyant attentiveness of Duke Boris, who – it was rumoured with some disbelief – had drunk champagne from the slipper of a chorus girl. He spent several weeks as a guest of Mrs Goelet, during which time May rode out with him on horseback or drove with him in an automobile without bothering to take a chaperone.

Three times he packed to leave and three times he changed his mind and stayed on. The excuse he released to the Press on the second occasion was that he had planned to travel on the Vanderbilt's yacht, but that it had broken down.

Nobody believed him. Everyone knew that Boris just wanted to stay near May. But while he was there, his volatile sensitivity caused a Society furore.

The Goelets and guests, including Boris, were invited to dine with Mrs Stuyvesant Fish, a formidable hostess, famed for her caustically vicious wit. Unfortunately one of her comments regarding Boris was brought to his attention, and caused him to take offence. With great posturing and loud protestations of deep hurt, the Russian count declared that he would not even drink soup with Mrs Fish, let alone step into her dining room as a dinner guest.

This left Mrs Goelet with a severe dilemma, for she had already accepted the invitation, but as Boris was residing in her house as a guest, she had no choice but to join him in refusing to go. Worse than that, she had to provide an alternative dinner.

Several mutual friends in that tightly-knit elite company had also accepted the original invitation but, valuing the status of Mrs Goelet and that of Count Boris, they sent their apologies to Mrs Fish in favour of the latter.

When Boris finally did leave, he left behind his cigarette box, possibly to provide an excuse to return yet again – particularly if one considers that his personal valet was responsible for making sure that all his master's property was collected and packed, and he, in turn, would be helped by the Goelet's household servants to identify and return any missed items in time for packing.

But May had obviously had enough and was not to be caught by this ruse. She sent on the box to Boris without delay.

He wrote back in his huge, flourishing handwriting:

Dear Miss May,

Thank you for having sent me back my cigarette box. I send you some cigarettes and a case for them that I hope you will like.

Believe me as your devoted friend.
Boris.

For May, this episode was the closure, not only of the Boris phase, but for that whole period of her life. She longed for stability and an end to the everlasting need to parry unwanted advances, both on herself and on her fortune.

She knew and was wary of every device for attempting to bring a man and woman together in the social matrimonial game. She saw through the flowery protestations of love; she lived daily with the awareness that in so many encounters she herself rated second to her immense fortune, and she had learned to dance the social rounds without serious entanglement, but she really loved any opportunity where she could meet people in a non- threatening atmosphere where she could just be herself.

In the August of 1903, such an opportunity occurred. It was at the America's Cup yacht race.

May's father, Ogden, who had died six years beforehand actually on his yacht, only days after attending Britain's most prestigious yachting week at Cowes, had always loved yacht racing. In fact, a world-renowned yachtsman in his own right, he had from 1882 to his death sponsored the Goelet Cup, an annual trophy race for yachtsmen competing in the Mediterranean, and its sporting value in America was compared to the Queen's Cup among the British yachting fraternity.

So yachting in all its forms had been part of May's life, and it was natural that she should attend the Americas Cup out of interest rather than a mere social distraction.

No doubt Kelso was aware of this and he chose to be there too. He knew that May had not been attracted by the more dashing and exotic suitors who had chased her around the world for the past eight years – including his friend Crichton. He knew, therefore, that unlike others, she was not looking for a title but for a true marriage. And apart from his title and estates, what he really had to offer her was his deep and genuine love.

Always a race that caused great rivalry between Britain and America, in 1903 there was even more hype than usual over the cup that year. The American yacht *Reliance* had caused a stir because she had several new and unique design features: her hull was much flatter than usual and had a fin-shaped keel that went very deep: she also sported the largest sail ever seen. Sir Thomas Lipton's British yacht *Shamrock III* was the latest design from Britain, and, even though it had had a couple of minor accidents en route across the Atlantic, it did pose a realistic challenge to *Reliant*. Hence, the rivalry was as intense as ever.

Lipton arrived on his personal yacht, *Erin,* which became the base for British hospitality throughout the trials, where he hosted all the other competitors and the important American dignitaries in attendance. However, the yacht used for American hospitality was none other than the *Mayflower*, which Mrs Goelet had sold after her husband's death.

By 1903 it had been bought as the Presidential yacht. A Reuter telegram on August 18th read: *'At the luncheon on board the Mayflower yesterday, Mr Roosevelt proposed the toast of the Great Powers and their sovereigns represented by Great Britain, Germany, Russia and Japan. The toast was drunk standing. The president went on to propose the health of the representatives of the International event.'* adding *'May the best boat win'*.

For May, visiting the *Mayflower* as a guest must have been very emotional, and that was something to which Kelso would be really sensitive. At her most vulnerable, she didn't need to seal herself in the shell she had encased herself in for protection against journalists and suitors. She was able to be just a woman. And to help their cause still further, after the opening ceremonials, the weather turned and they were beset by gale-force winds.

For the first time in its history, the race had to be postponed. Naturally, this extension of waiting time gave the two young people more time to get to know each other and to discover how much they had in common.

May, at last, discovered that she had met someone to whom she could safely show her true emotions. Kelso, in turn, realized that she was as insecure in matters of the heart as he was, and that she longed to meet someone she could trust.

May Goelet was at last falling in love and it was not long before the young man summoned the courage to propose.

This time, May said *yes*.

Mrs Goelet was ecstatic. She could see that, in the end, May had made the right choice – it was obvious that the two really loved each other – and yet he was a British duke. She had her wish.

Moreover, Kelso was a personal friend of the future king and his wife, and was not one of the mercenary, penniless ones who had pestered them for so long. Her satisfaction was complete when Kelso made it abundantly clear that he wanted no base financial settlement to sully *his* marriage. So she set about to arrange the *wedding of the year* and November was their chosen date.

In Scotland, Lady Anne, Kelso's mother, was also delighted that her son had finally found a bride. Concerned, at first, that she was not going to be able to make the journey to

New York for the wedding, she was desperately eager to welcome her future daughter-in-law and to assure her that she was coming to a beautiful new home, Floors Castle, and that there was a warm family waiting to take her to its heart.

Her first letter was sent from Broxmouth House, Dunbar, Scotland, her Dower House. This so clearly displayed the older lady's tact by implying that Floors was empty and awaiting its new mistress.

It reads:

Dearest May,

I must send you a few lines independent of my letter to my darling Boy to send my love and warmest wishes. I pray that you both be very happy together. When you know him better you will know what a treasure he is, so true and dependable and loving and I am sure he will do his best to make you happy. I hope you will get fond of us all. And believe that I will always love his wife. I wish you were over here, for I should have liked to have seen you so much but you must write to me which will make me realize it.

I hope you will love Floors as I love it and that together there may be many years of happiness in store for you – I want you to make Kelso happy for he does indeed deserve it.

Will you give your mother my love. Someday I will write to her – I can say no more except to assure you of the love and affection with which we will all receive you, dear May.

Very affectionately
A Roxburghe

In her delight and excitement, the duchess sent this letter with two-pence-ha'penny worth of stamps and May had to pay a surcharge of 10 cents.

The feminine bustle of trousseau preparation and wedding details were all too overwhelming for Kelso, and, no doubt, he found Mrs Goelet was too formidable a force at this critical point so on September 22nd he took off with friends for a hunting trip in the Rockies, accompanied by his friend and best-man-to-be, the Honourable Reginald Ward, brother of Lord Dudley.

While there, he kept a diary, scribbled in pencil on notepaper, firstly from *Buffalo Bill's Barn* and later from *Cody's Hotel*, which he boasted was '*strictly 1st class and Modern. Rates $3 per day and upwards*'.

> The diary reads as follows:
> *'Tuesday 22nd September*
> *Arrived Cody. Fixed up packs and bought a few things.*
> *Wed 23rd*
> *Driven by Gus Thompson 55 miles to valley, lunching and changing horses at T.T. Ranche. Col. Cody's 38 miles – found hunter & man waiting with packs etc.*
> *Thurs 24th*
> *Up early, got packs fixed up and left valley 9am crossing divide about 2pm and camping about 4pm*
> *– a little snow about but warm in daytime. Trail bad.*
> *Fri 25th*
> *After good night, not so cold as I expected, got packs on – had snap at small elk from trail but no result. Reached camp on Thorofare Creek at 12 o'clock. Started out about 1 o'clock and took turn round back of camp. Only saw a few cows. Got back, rain turning to snow during the night.*

V, cold.
Sat. 26th
Started out 9.30 and after stiffish walk roused single bull – went on and eventually roused another, which I got after much fusilading – nice head 12 points – Back to camp 4pm. Reg had gone off after big bull that had come down across the flat close to camp – Harold having gone to bring in his head went on hunting – Camp quite comfortable in edge of timber – we have capital tent and are quite comfy but nights are v. cold.
Think we should have good sport as game seems plentiful but Harold has been rousting them up well.
Harold shot nice 12 pointer on way back to camp – Reg had no success after the big one.
Sun. 27th
Harold and I went out and fetched our heads riding both ways. Mine turned out to be equal if not better than Harold's. Reg came in v. late having got capital beast with very curious head.
Mon 28th
Harold & I went together & watched a lot he eventually shooting nice beast – I made back to camp but saw nothing – Dispatch rider in camp but alas no mail.
Tues 28th
Out with Harold saw lots of beasts in heavy timbered creek but could do no good with them as weather was snowy & thick and wind bad. Reg did not get a shot.
Wed 29th
Davies goes into valley with letters. Dirty wet morning. After lunch Reg & I went out Harold taking a day off.

Eventually saw a good lot of beasts & went down but to my horror found Reg was already crawling in on them. Crept down back of a ridge and waited and after Reg shot, a fine 14 pointer came to me which I got. Reg had killed good 12 pointer & wounded 10 pointer which he afterwards got.
Thurs 30th
Men went out to collect beasts – took the morning off. Harold & I going out after lunch spying for sheep with no success and went looking at beaver dams and houses.
Fri 1st October
Davies arrived last night but to our disappointment no letters only a telegram from Buck Barclay about Gaddesby – can't make out what has happened. He must go off again today and if no letters at Valley go right through to Cody.

On the back of Friday's page, there was a list of items which obviously made the expedition more comfortable:
Bed legs, Camp chairs
Books, Nailed shoes
Spats, Jaegar Sleeping Suit
Short fur coat, Fur rug
Stalking rug
Fri. 1st Oct contd.
Davies left early with letters and telegrams for Cody. The cook was given the sack but could not find his horse so stayed over a day. Snowy and thick all 3 went out after lunch & walked the wood for blacktail which horse man had seen but no success.

Sat 2nd Oct
More snow and high winds during the night but started out for sheep. Long hard walk with no results – Heard Harold have shot early and found he had got good ram on return to camp. Snow squalls all day. Reg rode out but came straight back.

Sun 3rd Oct
More snow and high winds during the night. Harold and I did not go out. Reg started out after lunch to try and get a blacktail but no success.

Mon 4th Oct
All 3 started out in various directions for sheep – I had long day and in places v. tricky walking – all came back empty incessant snow showers making regular hunting difficult. Weather looks as snowy as ever but hope for change.

Tues 5th Oct
Last night we had a gale and a snowstorm, tent only just surviving – gale and snow showers went on during the day so useless even to start out – expecting Davies with letters but fear he has put it off. Wish I had been spending this day with May for her birthday.

Wed 6th Oct
Went out in three detachments but with no success except Brassey who got a nice ram. To our joy Davies arrived 11.30pm after bad journey in snow. Delighted with letters but dejected at sad news in telegram – slept badly in consequence. (this was probably news of the death of May's uncle)

Thurs 7th Oct

Had a long day but again no success – in early, writing and telegraphing. V. tired after two long days walking bad in drifting snow.
Fri 8th Oct
Went out with Kipford, Brassey coming with us. After long stiff walk on to ridge below camp and spied sheep lying on opposite face. Stalked down and on way found fresh trail of big ones – Kipford looking round saw one 150 yards away up hill watching us, sat down and plugged him. Then waited and saw two others 170 yards off, took the lowest one and hit him first shot and found him dead 200 yards down the hill. Both had good heads fifteen and three quarter inches – had stiff walk back to camp carrying two heads but rejoice at success after 5 v. hard days.
Sat 9th Oct
Reg went out with Kepford for sheep but no success. Meant to take day off but men in getting horses located some deer. Harold and I went out, he having hard galloping, shot in timber. We went on and I shot fair buck v. easy shot.
Sun. 10th Oct
Moved camp big job; got off about 12 and into new place where we had to scrape snow away, about 5.30 more again tomorrow over divide so rather piggy night but not cold.
Mon 11th Oct
Moved camp over the divide. Got off earlier and into camp earlier. Much warmer this side and no snow v. comfortable. Davies goes off tomorrow – write my last

letters and telegrams from the wilds.

On this sheet there is the draft of part of a letter to May discussing the wedding:-

'And Isobel will come out but I doubt Alasdair coming when the time comes. I am counting the days and shall be back with you soon after you get this which I hope will cheer you up – Goodbye now, my Darling, God bless you and keep you. You can't think how I can have enjoyed this trip with only the one feeling that I ought really to have gone home or stayed with you.

Your own loving,

Bumble – Bumble is the nickname Kelso had been given, probably at Sandhurst, and it was certainly what Prince George always called him.

Tues 12th Oct
Glorious warm day. Reg and Kepford went off with pack horses & tent to camp higher up for sheep. I went up creek, Harold going down in search of blacktail. Came back early as was disgusted with thick timber and closeness of country. Little chance of spying game & shooting except snapshots.
Wed 13th Oct
Much colder – both started down creek riding in search of more open country but snow coming on both came back early – came on to fresh trail of deer that had winded us on way home but tracks bad to follow in the snow.
Thurs. 14th Oct
Started early with gt hopes of success on account of

yesterday's snow but had v. long day and no result. Don't fancy this a good deer country. Reg didn't come so don't move tomorrow.

Fri 15th Oct

Harold and I took it easy in morning read letters and papers Davies brought in last night. Took a turn out in the evening but as feared no success. Reg arrived back with Kepford with nothing.

Sat 16th Oct

Moved camp to T.E.Ranche my last day so went on with Kepford ahead and hunted near them but again no good and must be satisfied with one blacktail. Pack arrived v. late, had capital supper & bed in ranch (1st for 1 month!)

Sun 17th Oct Left T.E. Ranche about 9 and reach Cody 3.30 Davies driving me in. Reg & Harold moved camp to Table Mt & leave Cody 22nd for Winnipeg. Found capital mail and lots of letters. Spent some time washing, shaving, packing and telegraphing. Joined train 8.45 after capital supper. Enjoyed trip v. much.

Mon 18th Oct. In train was extravagant & had state room – posted note back to Reg with some letters.

Meanwhile, much had been happening in New York in Kelso's absence.

May had answered her future mother-in-law's letter and had received another warm response, this time from the Grosvenor Street address in London:

Dearest May,

Your letter pleased me so much. Indeed dear, I think of you both so much and it makes me happy to get Kelso's happy letters. I am sure that I will love you for your own sake as well as for his, and it will be a great happiness to me if you grow fond of us all as I hope you will. We have always been all so much to one another, and to me I hope you will always be one of the family.

You will be missing Kelso dreadfully (while away camping) *am sorry for you parted for I know what it is and I can't help thinking from his letter today that he may after all chuck the sport and come back to you – for he seemed very lonely and miserable without you. But you must have a great deal to do and perhaps you will get through better if he is away.*

It must be very difficult ordering your trousseau at a distance as I suppose you are getting it in Paris, and I do feel for you leaving your own country when you marry, but please do not feel you are coming among strangers, for we are all ready to welcome you at Floors. It is so bright and sunny and lovely and I hope it may be to you the same blissful home it has always been to me.'

In truth, Lady Anne knew it was not in Kelso's character to give up any undertaking, despite loneliness and unhappiness, but she was kindly expressing to May that her son had confided to her in his letters how much he was missing his fiancée. Although she most certainly had seen May at many social functions, she was longing to meet her as her future daughter-in-law, and was much frustrated that it seemed at first that she would not be able to get to the ceremony.

This problem was resolved when the wedding had to be delayed a week, which enabled the duchess and her daughter, Lady Isobel, to set off for Liverpool where they boarded the Cunard liner, *Campania,* en route for New York.

The reason for the delay was that May's uncle, Sir Michael (Minga) Herbert, brother of the Duke of Pembroke, had suddenly died. This was probably the news in the telegram that had distressed Kelso on his trip.

Because of the very rigid observation of mourning etiquette in the Victorian/Edwardian period, this was to change the whole wedding by imposing certain restrictions. No longer could it be a celebration for all of the cream of New York's Society plus visiting aristocracy, for it must now be restricted to family members and very close friends only – a mere 250!

To Mrs Goelet, this was catastrophic, with her dreams of the most dazzling wedding ever staged in New York being dashed. Nevertheless, she stoically adjusted her plans, never guessing that the obligatory reduction in the guest list was to result in an event which was to make May's wedding memorable for a far more unique, if ignominious, reason.

Lady Anne responded to the news with great sympathy, but in her letter of condolence to May, she added '*I hope that it will not make any difference as regards your wedding – though you may have it quieter probably which will be a great comfort to Kelso*'.

How well she knew her son. The prospect of a simpler wedding was very pleasing to Kelso, to whom large events were more duty than pleasure. He was also delighted that the deferred date meant that his mother and Isobel were able to come to New York after all, and he made no effort to hide his joyful anticipation of meeting them when their boat docked.

Chapter 9
Final Wedding Preparations

For Kelso, the real preparation for the wedding actually began when he arrived at the dock to meet the *Campania* but his natural reticence and years in the strictly regulated service of the Royal Family left him totally unprepared for the overwhelming clamour of journalists and photographers lying in wait for him on the quayside.

Unaware that it was the custom for a liner to telegraph the passenger list through to the major newspapers from about sixty miles east of berth to alert them of notables on board, he had no idea that anyone but his immediate family should know the date, let alone the actual time of their arrival.

But, once the names of the Duchess of Roxburghe and her daughter, Lady Isobel, had been flagged up in the newsrooms of New York, every paper wanted to be there to get the first pictures and any minutiae they could glean about the Roxburghes, the Goelets, and the coming marriage.

Therefore, as the bridegroom's car drew up and he stepped out, unaccompanied, he was mobbed by frantic reporters, each vying with each other to quiz him.

Their first questions were about where May was and why she hadn't joined him to meet her future mother-in-law; they quizzed him as to why not one of the Goelets was present, not even his future brother-in-law, Robert; they were desperate to discover where his mother and sister were to stay – and a whole barrage of personal things, all of which Kelso thought were intrusively impertinent.

He pushed through the throng, answering curtly that in Britain it was not customary to discuss one's personal affairs with the press, and that he had chosen to meet his family alone. Then he pushed through onto the quayside itself into an area forbidden to them, and seemed apparently unaware that he was still in range of their cameras.

Frustrated, they watched the athletic, handsome young duke, dressed in a double-breasted serge suit, Derby hat and fawn-coloured overcoat, pacing impatiently up and down, swinging his light walking cane and occasionally tugging his moustache.

The reporters were to romanticize that Kelso's agitation was due to the fact that he had so missed his family that he could not wait to see them, and this was exacerbated by the fact that the liner, having hit bad weather on the crossing, had difficulty manoeuvring and took a full hour to berth.

Indeed, Kelso was longing for a reunion with his mother and Isobel, but his agitation was caused far more by the irritation he felt at being under constant intense scrutiny from the press.

The moment the gang plank touched the quayside, he leapt onto it and ran up past the startled stewards. He gave his mother and sister huge bear hugs before following them below to their state rooms. The reporters commented later that the Roxburghe greeting was '*very affectionate*' and that they were a '*very devoted family*'.

Whether Lady Anne asked about the gaggle of reporters she had seen from deck, or whether Kelso discussed with her his annoyance at their persistence is unclear, but the duchess felt it wiser to satisfy them with a brief interview. She persuaded her son to admit them and that, as her arrival was the target of their present interest, she herself had no problem in meeting them on her own terms.

Thus, having reluctantly accepted that all they'd get that day was a fleeting glimpse of the noble visitors, the representatives from the press were astounded to be suddenly invited on board and conducted to the reception room, where the duchess and her daughter charmingly received them, while Kelso stood in attendance.

They saw an elegant, gracious lady who sat with the easy dignity of one who had spent long years in the Court of the late queen. She was a fine-looking, well-built woman with greying hair under a purple picture hat with its veil turned back. She was dressed in a tight-fitting mink jacket or *sacque*, with a wealth of white and yellow lace at her neck and down the front of her corsage. Her grey woollen skirt was described as '*elaborately designed but simple in* effect', and she carried a muff. There was a noticeable resemblance between her and her son who stood in silence nearby. Lady Isobel was striking too with an even stronger likeness to her brother but with darker colouring.

She sat beside her mother, dressed in a tight-fitting sable bolo jacket with a thick travelling skirt of a '*yellowish-brown material*' and russet shoes. She wore a '*high, upturned felt*' hat.

Kelso now appeared totally at ease, obviously confident

in his mother's ability to handle the situation. She herself was full of charm and captivated her inquisitors instantly, while at the same time managing to parry their more intrusive questions with the skill of a seasoned courtier.

Their first aim was to glean from her what they had failed to discover from Kelso, namely where they would be staying. With an air of surprised innocence, she admitted to having left all such details to her son and thereby managed to make any further enquiry on the subject seem impolite. It was the same with intimate questions about the wedding arrangements, so they changed tack and quoted recent, rather offensive articles in the American Press, which had more than suggested that American brides of aristocrats had been coldly received in Britain, although their fortunes had not.

Seemingly unaware of the insinuation and oblivious of any intention to offend, Lady Anne smiled sweetly and answered: *'Oh dear me, no!'*

She then explained with disarming directness that in Britain marriage was not seen merely as a financial arrangement, but that these young men had *'an extreme fondness for their brides'*. She followed this with a denial that young American heiress-brides were unwelcome in Society, saying; *'Why, of course we welcome them, and they are very happy, which is shown by the number of American girls who are now with titled husbands in England'*.

At this point, Kelso indicated that the interview was over and dismissed the Press delegation. He also sent instructions for the waiting car to be brought round to the rear entrance of the pier, which he had noticed was covered and would offer more privacy.

Even so, they waited until most of the passengers had disembarked and then the Roxburghes thanked the captain and made for the gangway, where the tenacity of several photographers paid off and their farewells and hasty clambering into the automobile were caught on camera. The driver then whisked them away from any further intrusion to the privacy of the Savoy.

Inevitably, however, it was huge news in New York that Lady Anne, Duchess of Roxburghe, and Lady Isobel Innes-Kerr were in town for the Goelet wedding. Indeed, the Press had already suggested that Lady Isobel may be one of the bridesmaids.

Then their stature was even more enhanced when it was learned that Mrs Astor, *'The Hostess par Excellence of New York',* took the unprecedented step of rearranging her diary so that she could entertain the Dowager Duchess of Roxburghe. *The* Mrs Astor, who was director and principal indicator of every *Season,* changed her calendar and inaugurated the Winter Season early that year, exclusively for Her Grace, the Dowager Duchess of Roxburghe, because her schedule demanded that she should return to Britain on the *Campania* almost immediately after the wedding, and thus would not have been available on the date originally set aside by Mrs Astor.

It was recorded in the Press, with awe, as one of the rare occasions that Mrs Astor actually changed her plans and it took Society totally by surprise, as many had not yet returned to New York, having set their diaries by the previously issued 'Astor timetable'.

Nevertheless, she laid on one of her inimitable dinner

parties to welcome the duchess and to introduce her to a select group of twenty-six of America's elite inner circle, which inevitably included newly-met and soon-to-be family members such as Mrs Goelet, her son Robert, her brother Orme Wilson and his wife, Caroline Astor (Mrs Astor's own daughter), plus their sister, Grace, and her husband, Cornelius Vanderbilt.

Dinner was set in the great dining room, which was hung with priceless tapestries. There was just one very long table at the centre of which sat their hostess, and Lady Anne, as guest of honour, was placed directly opposite to her.

The Astor's fabled gold dinner service was laid out, and three great golden vases were filled with exceptionally large but absolutely perfect pink and white chrysanthemums. At each lady's place was a corsage of American Beauty roses, while the gentlemen received white carnations. The drawing room and the ballroom were adorned by exuberant displays of American Beauty roses and exotic palms.

As was her custom, Mrs Astor wore her famous emeralds and diamonds, and, predictably for her, she chose a dress in emerald velvet trimmed in sable to complement them. Dressed thus, she felt *herself* and therefore comfortable to emanate, as always, the confidence of America's *queen of hostesses,* even for so elevated a guest as the Dowager Duchess of Roxburghe.

After the meal, the company retired to the ballroom where coffee was served although, as the evening had been convened in such haste, there was no music or entertainment.

Their American hosts were determined to make sure that the ladies, and their escort, Captain Reginald Ward, Kelso's best man, were to see as much of New York as possible in their brief visit. Somehow, they successfully managed an itinerary, which avoided too much interference from the Press and afford the guests a real taste of life in the great city.

Mrs Goelet took them by car to the Brooklyn Bridge where they then joined the thronging crowds, on foot, to explore Park Row and Lower Broadway.

They later crossed over Printing House Square to the Post Office, where Lady Anne was fascinated by the huge bulletin board displaying topical pictures. From there, they went to view the Park Row Building, their first experience of a skyscraper at close quarters.

Having gazed from below at its dizzying heights, they went in where Captain Ward stayed with Her Grace on ground level, while the others went up in one of the new express elevators to view the city from the top floor.

Then they mingled again with the crowd as they went towards Broadway. They went as far as Ann Street, where they boarded a Broadway car to continue their journey to the Empire Building, where they met up with Mrs Goelet's brother, T.R. Wilson Jnr, who escorted them to Wall Street itself.

He took them into the new Stock Exchange building through a side entrance and up to the gallery, from which they could see the hectic dealings below, which Wilson tried to explain as simply as he could. They seemed interested and asked many questions.

He then led them to a private gallery, which necessitated crossing a corner of the actual Exchange floor, which the Press made much of later as they were they very first women to do so while trading was in session in the new building.

At the end of their visit they were conducted out of the main building, where they paused to observe the impressive front facade, before climbing into T.R's waiting automobile and taken home.

Chapter 10
The Wedding

Over the next few days, Kelso was to discover that the experience on the quayside was mild compared with what was to come. He still expected to go about his affairs as normal, but this was out of the question.

A crowd of close on 300 had set themselves up outside 608 Fifth Avenue, May's home, in addition to the many reporters and photographers, all eager to catch a glimpse of a real live duke; and – better still – of the happy couple together.

Kelso was totally adamant that he would not forfeit his privacy, whatever the pressure, and, when he arrived to visit May, he barely waited for his brougham to stop before leaping out and dashing up the steps, ignoring all questions.

Nevertheless, he couldn't help overhearing the comments such as *'Why, he looks just like other folks, doesn't he?'* before he reached the haven of the door, flushed and angry.

Later, when he took May and his sister Isobel for a drive in Central Park, again they had to run the gauntlet both on the way out and on the way back.

But, if the crowds felt cheated of their principal prize, they were rewarded with the sight of a non-stop flow of the great and famous as they called on the Goelets to deposit their gifts. It seemed as if all the famed *Four Hundred* from the most elite of American Society wanted to be seen at no. 608 during those few days, and it was already rumoured that the value of the wedding presents exceeded a million dollars and were worth more than those of any other bride to date.

Two days before the wedding, the general flow of guests calmed down somewhat as Mrs Goelet set about the final preparations for the wedding. She left in the morning to check that the church was ready. En route, her 'electric car' broke down twice, but she finally managed to get there. Because of the serious down-sizing of the guest-list, she had employed the finest florists in New York to transform what was, in reality, a cathedral-sized church into what she liked to call a *'little English chapel'*. She wanted whole areas cordoned off and obscured by thousands of shrubs and flowers to create an intimate area in which the wedding would be enacted.

That day, May stayed home, and Kelso, after setting off after breakfast for a short spin in a hired electric cab, abandoned it when it too broke down, and took a short walk instead before returning to the Savoy to have lunch, then to escort his mother and sister to visit his fiancée.

This time, the hired electric brougham took them safely and directly to the Goelet's.

About an hour later, they were joined by Mrs Astor and her daughter, Mrs R.T. Wilson, and her son and daughter-in-law, together with the Cornelius Vanderbilts for what was described as an 'informal gathering', where they were able to view the wedding presents and the wonderful flowers by now adorning the whole house.

At six, the Roxburghes returned to the Savoy to rest and dress in time to be taken back to 608 for dinner at 8.30, with a mere fourteen intimate family and friends.

Two rehearsals were scheduled for the following day at St Thomas' Church, one at 1pm and the other at four. Although there had been much secrecy over these times, a hopeful crowd gathered early in expectation.

By now, Kelso's soldier's instinct took over and he out-manoeuvred them by finding an unobtrusive rear entrance to the church and entered unobserved.

The crowd was large, in spite of the fact that May's brother Robert had complained to the police about the persistence of the Press, particularly after he had actually chased one photographer for half a block down 5th Avenue on the previous day for snapping his camera in May's face as she entered her carriage.

A few more officers had been deployed but their presence was barely felt as the excitement of the waiting crowd escalated with every arrival. But excitement escalated when at 4.15 precisely, the cream-coloured livery of the Goelet coach was seen bringing May and her mother a little after the others.

The bride-to-be was dressed in black with a corsage of lilies of the valley. She hurried past the frustrated photographers, holding her muff over her face and saying: *'O don't take my picture!'* and ran up the steps into the church behind her mother who totally ignored the crowd.

The rehearsal lasted more than an hour during which time Mrs Goelet herself directed three complete practices of the ceremony, every detail of which she had devised, including several unique features which broke with normal traditions.

One such was that she had decided to remove the ushers from the actual bridal procession, so that instead of escorting the bridesmaids they would march up the aisle in pairs when it was time to do so and take up their places in the pews, leaving the choir to lead in the bridesmaids and the bride.

Eventually, the party left the church to be carried away swiftly in their carriages, while the choir stayed on for a further hour or so to practice the hymns, together with the organist and harpist who would be accompanying them.

Everyone else, namely the immediate families, the bridesmaids and the ushers, returned to 608 Park Avenue, where there was to be an early dinner just for them so that they could all have a good rest before the following day's celebration.

*****

The wedding day dawned fair and although the ceremony itself was not until 2pm, the crowds of eager sightseers began to build up quite early. They were joined by a new group of ladies who were determined to get into the church to see what was going on. Some of these had hoped to be on the guest list before the family's bereavement, and they confidently thought they could talk themselves in anyway. So it was that some actually persuaded the sexton and a couple of workmen finishing off the preparations to allow them into the gallery.

May's cousin, Robert Wilson Goelet, one of the ushers posted on duty early, realised what was happening and approached the ladies to request them to leave. But, having got this far, they were not prepared to give up. Protesting that they had the sexton's permission, they point blank refused to go.

Robert threatened to call the police. Appalled, an indignant Sexton Williams, eager to remove blame from himself, pleaded with the Rector, Reverend Stires, on behalf of the interlopers.

But the Rector knew only too well what Mrs Ogden Goelet would expect, and sided strongly with Robert.

The police arrived and politely but firmly ejected the irate ladies. After this, Robert and his friends decided it would be as well to check the whole church and actually found three more who had hidden themselves at the top of a small staircase. They, too, were required to leave.

Seemingly undaunted, several looked for other means of access, as all doors were then well locked until the ceremony. Some spotted the coal delivery chutes around the side of the building. They reasoned that if the coal was delivered there, then there must be an internal passage through which it would be transported to the furnaces. This, in turn, must lead into the church itself.

So they prised off the man-hole covers and proceeded to ease themselves down the hole. But, by now, the few police on duty were more vigilant, and they were assisted by the fact that elegant Edwardian dresses, complete with bustles, did not go easily through grimy rings in the ground, no matter how slim and athletic the young ladies attempting to achieve this feat were. They were hauled out as politely as possible in such an absurd situation and, once more, turned away.

Thus, further thwarted by the police, these ladies became very angry. They were unaccustomed to being opposed at all, let alone by the constabulary, whom they considered as mere public servants – or in other words *their* servants.

The police, too, were at a loss, for never before had they been called upon to physically control ladies of the upper class.

As an Inspector McLaughlin said on behalf of the police, to the Press later – of course they knew how to contain a riot – *'but not when it was run by educated ladies dressed in expensive costumes'*.

But, by now, the growing anger was fuelling the beginnings of a riot. The inspector, as duty officer, was trying to control things with a group of only ten men. He sent repeatedly for reinforcements, but they were very slow in coming as no-one could have anticipated such an occurrence.

He knew that some of the women in the crowd were dressmakers, and he had sympathy with them, knowing they needed to see the bride's dress so that they could go straight home to recreate it, either for their own customers or for those of their mistress. This was their livelihood.

He had less sympathy with the reporters and photographers, as he was convinced their attitude to folks caused negative reactions. He was familiar with dealing with sightseers, who generally were a good-natured enough bunch, and responded to easy policing, but this added dimension of arrogant and angry so-called *gentle-women* had definitely disturbed the balance, and the overall tone was turning decidedly ugly.

The appearance of a coach with white ribbons and cockades on both the horses and the coachmen, plus the cream Goelet livery, triggered a forward surge from the crowd in expectation that this might be the bride.

The police moved and managed to force them back as the coach slowed down, and the startled faces of Mrs Goelet and the Dowager Duchess of Roxburghe stared out.

The disappointment caused a momentary lull, which

allowed the next three coaches to force their way in behind with some difficulty, and from two of these the bridesmaids stepped out and were glimpsed briefly, before they disappeared under the awning which had been erected, leading up to the main door of the church. Sufficient was seen to excite the crowd, and they once more surged forward to try for a better view.

At this point, an open carriage tried to push its way through. It was Mr and Mrs Cornelius Vanderbilt, who had their two little daughters sitting on the front seat. Some of the women pressed against the carriage to admire the children, but the police grabbed them to force them back, and in the scuffle that followed, the confusion of long dresses and feathered hats became so alarming that, with a shout to his driver, Cornelius stepped down from the carriage, helped his wife and elder daughter down, before lifting the tearful younger child in his arms, and shepherding them, and hurried the rest of the way on foot.

Angered by the police response, and aware now that the next carriage would surely be the bride's, the crowd turned to meet it.

They were right. The horses were decorated with enormous streamers of white ribbons, with cockades of white ribbons and lilies of the valley. The coachmen and footmen also wore white cockades, but instead of wearing the Goelet cream, they were dressed in the duke's livery of dark blue broadcloth, with gold-buttoned coats and vests. They wore trousers which reached just below knee level, and were fastened with a strap over white silk stockings, while their shoes were fastened with gold buckles.

The carriage was brought to an abrupt halt. May, who was making final adjustments with the help of her hand mirror, was suddenly surrounded by clamouring women, who jumped onto the carriage steps to see her better, and even reached in to feel the material of her dress.

Terrified, she cowered away from the grasping hands, and her brother, Robert, leapt up to push them away as he screamed for the police to help.

Most were unable to do more than grapple with a few women, but the one mounted officer present realised the situation and responded by riding his horse directly towards the immobilised coach, and, for fear of being trampled, the women had to back off, allowing the other police officers to close in and thus help to get the carriage to the church entrance during the brief hiatus.

At last, May was out of the carriage.

Even then one resourceful cameraman jumped onto the back axle of the coach in a final attempt to get a shot, but he was instantly dragged off by police.

The whole episode had caused a fifteen minute delay, but at last she was out of the carriage and about to enter the church, when there was yet another scuffle as an officer grabbed a woman from the rear as she tried to crawl under the awning to catch a glimpse of the bride.

To his horror, he found her to be at least sixty years old and covered with dust from her efforts.

The newspapers the following day were full of righteous indignation and horror at what had happened, deploring the women's violent intrusions into '*the New York girl's wedding*' saying:

'Never before in the history of the city, it was agreed, had the city's sense of decency been so outraged, or the spirit of democracy so humbled'. Failing to mention, of course their own contribution to the chaos.

Later, they interviewed several ladies of a more genteel disposition, who added their condemnation to such chaos. Among these was Frances Hodgeson Burnett, author of '*Little Lord Fauntleroy*', the little half-American boy who becomes an earl.

One report reads:

'Women Beat Policemen

Bystanders support the Inspector in his statements. There were innumerable instances where the women fiercely beat the policemen with their clenched fists and had to be carried, kicking and screaming from the front of the church.

'The task of the policemen was made immeasurably worse by the fact that many of the most persistent women were refined and intelligent in appearance, well dressed and apparently of the highest respectability.

'Feeling that the seven thousand women who thus forgot their sex, as well as the consideration deserved by their kind, and the American spirit that holds in contempt all worship of rank and title, were not representative of the womanhood of New York.'

The American

*****

After this traumatic experience, May was given a few moments to compose herself, while within the church, Kelso, who had repeated the previous day's ploy and slipped in with his best man through the back entrance, was anxiously waiting.

Aware that there was a time delay, he was unaware of the ordeal that his bride had just endured.

The church itself was an oasis of calm. The organist had been playing music from Lohengrin, followed by selections from Gounod's *Romeo and Juliet,* including a duet for organ and harp; Schubert's *Ave Maria,* followed by Brousseau's *Elevation.* And while they enjoyed the music, the guests could marvel at the way that the vast church had been transformed into a chapel of flowers. The whole body of the church, except the nave, had been screened off by towering palms and ferns, which also blocked off all pews that did not open onto the centre aisle. Smaller palms screened the choristers' stalls, through which it was possible to see the ropes of white roses with which the stalls and chancel rail were hung.

English ivy was entwined round the grey stone columns along the north and south sides of the nave, giving the impression of climbing up towards the great baskets which hung from the capitals, in which primroses and specially forced may-blossom grew. At the entrance to every pew there was a knot of white chrysanthemums and white roses against a spray of plumed asparagus. The transept itself seemed like a palm garden, in which orchids, roses, lilies of the valley and white chrysanthemums bloomed, and the altar was dressed in tall white lilies in huge vases.

The Dowager Duchess of Roxburghe sat in the front pew on one side of the aisle, and Mrs Goelet in the front pew on the other side. Her Grace was dressed in a gown of wine-coloured velvet and wore a hat that was compared to one in a painting by Gainsborough. Mrs Goelet wore a costume of Nile-green panne velvet, elaborately embroidered with seed pearls and Point d'Alencon lace, with a matching toque trimmed in white lace and sable.

The ushers were waiting at the entrance, and each wore a white cravat fixed with Kelso's gift, which was a souvenir pin bearing his and May's initials, set in small diamonds and surmounted by a coronet of sapphires, rubies and diamonds.

Two of them were British friends of Kelso, the Honourable Hugh Baring and Harold Brassey, and the others were Robert Wilson Goelet, William Woodward, Henry Rodgers Winthrop, and Henry Worthington Bull.

Once they were assured that May had recovered enough to begin her procession, they went up the aisle in formation, as planned, and took their seats.

At this point, Kelso and his best man, the Honourable Reginald Ward, brother of Lord Dudley, each wearing buttonholes of gardenias, came from the vestry with Bishop Doane of Albany, and the Rector of St Thomas', Reverend Dr Stires.

The bridegroom and his best man were both dressed in black frock jackets, grey trousers and white waistcoats. Kelso's white silk Ascot tie was held by a single grey pearl, and both carried pearl-grey gloves and silk top hats.

Once they were in place, a procession of fifty choristers walked down the aisle to meet the bridal party, singing *O Perfect Love,* and, on arrival, turned and processed back, followed, twenty paces behind, by the bridesmaids, behind whom walked May, led by her brother, Robert.

The eight bridesmaids were dressed in pink mousseline de

soie, – silk muslin – dresses, edged in ecru lace, decorated just below the waistline with a basket of flowers, worked in raised embroidery. Over the dresses, they wore coats in Louis XV style, made of lace and chiffon. Their headdresses were toques of velvet in the same shade of pink, edged with sable, trimmed with feathers, and each young lady carried a muff in matching sable and velvet, decorated with clusters of pink roses – pink being May's favourite colour.

Lady Isobel and Miss Beatrice Mills led the procession, followed by Miss Nina Thayer, Miss Alice Babcock, Miss Marian Haven, Miss Martha Johnson, Miss Therese Iselin and Miss Pauline Whittier, in pairs.

Twenty paces behind and leaning on her brother's arm, came the tiny figure of May. Her gown was made of priceless English point lace, over a heavy white satin under-dress, covered in tulle, which supported the lace, giving a fluffy effect. The skirt was decorated with garlands of British hawthorne – or Mayflower, for her name – with trails of orange blossom. The bodice was high-necked, with sleeves of lace and was trimmed with old lace. Her long veil, over a very long train, was attached by an orange-blossom headdress, and she carried an ivory-bound prayer book, on which was pinned a small bouquet of gardenias, orchids and Scottish heather.

As May approached the chancel steps, she paused and Kelso walked down to meet her, then turning, he led her through the double line of bridesmaids to take up position in front of the Bishop and Reverend Stires for the opening part of the ceremony, after which they moved to the chancel rail, while Reverend Stires read the service.

This was followed by Bishop Doane pronouncing the

blessing, to which the choir sang Stainer's sevenfold *Amen*.

Then the clergy, the bride and groom, the Dowager Duchess of Roxburghe, Mrs Goelet, Lady Isobel, the best man and Mrs Cornelius Vanderbilt, – who had sat with Her Grace throughout – all went into the vestry, '*as was the British custom*', to sign the register.

Kelso signed Henry John, Duke of Roxburghe; the bride signed her full maiden name; Lady Anne signed Annie Roxburghe, and the other signatories were Mrs Goelet, Captain Ward and Robert Goelet.

As they returned to the altar, the choir was singing *To Thee, Oh Father*, then the bridal pair walked down the aisle to a triumphant rendering of Mendelssohn's *Wedding March*.

As they left the church, May was all smiles, while Kelso, the press reported, looked more serious, anxious no doubt about escorting May safely through to their carriage.

The crowds were still there, hoping for a glimpse of the bride and they erupted in delight when the duke and his new duchess appeared, but they were hastily hustled into their carriage which forced its way through towards Fifth Avenue with the help of the extra police who had finally arrived. But many of their guests, seeing the pressure of the rioting women decided it to be unsafe to attempt to travel by coach and set off on foot to walk the four blocks instead.

Once the bride and groom and their guests were safely out of the way, the police, in the hope of diffusing the situation, made the decision to allow people in to see the church. But this crowd was beyond appeasement, and it swarmed all over, stripping the aisles of any floral decorations that could be reached and torn down.

At this, the police, realizing their mistake, re-formed and drove everybody out and had the doors locked behind them.

But for May and Kelso, this nightmare was over. They stood serenely in the bay window of the drawing room to receive their guests, surrounded by mauve orchids and ferns, which spilled through into the library. The hall and grand staircase were decked in American Beauty Roses and yellow orchids.

A buffet luncheon was served in the conservatory, and the wedding breakfast itself in the dining room on the Goelet's gold dinner service, which was enhanced by liberty roses in beautiful gold vases. The wedding cake was in two tiers and had been made concealing favours, in line with the old traditions; namely, two rings, which if found by a man and maid denoted they would marry within the year. There was a thimble for the lady destined to be an old maid, a button for the eternal bachelor and a 6d for good luck.

May herself distributed the cake in little white moire silk boxes with the initials G&R intertwined beneath a ducal crown, and although recipients of the favours were supposed to conceal their finds, the search led to much merriment.

As the bride and groom were scheduled to leave at 5pm, the reception was not very long. May changed into her going-away outfit of silver-grey cloth and velvet in the identical shade of grey, embroidered in gold, with a hat to match, and, although they planned a hasty exit for the couple for fear of any further crowd problems, the ushers still stole out while they were making their farewells, and decorated the coach with white satin streamers.

Again, it was a laughing May who ran down the steps to

her coach, followed by a more serious Kelso, trying in vain to dodge the showers of rice thrown by the ushers.

Robert Goelet and Reginald Ward drove ahead of them to Grand Central Station to clear the way, and a mounted policeman led the carriage which drove off at speed, with May waving merrily to her bridesmaids, who were all waving from windows. As they left, someone threw a white slipper which landed on the roof of the carriage and stuck there until they reached the corner of 45th Street and Madison Avenue, where it was flung off, only to be retrieved by a young boy called Isadore Grebman, who grabbed it, hid it in his shirt, and set off for the station where, although he was too late to catch May, he '*opened negotiations for the sale of the slipper'* with Robert Goelet.

Meanwhile, May and Kelso had entered the Vanderbilt entrance of the station, where they left the coach and ran through the main concourse outside the waiting room. There, the station employees and some commuters made a 'lane' for them to pass through quickly to catch the 5pm Boston train, onto which had been added a private car for them. They were travelling to Newport where they were to spend the first weeks of their honeymoon at Ochre Court, the Goelet's sumptuous holiday mansion on the cliffs of Rhode Island.

Preparations at Ochre Court had been at fever-pitch for days, and it was reported that chefs had been working since the early hours, even by gaslight. The festivities were set to continue there for some days, as the young couple were to be joined in due course by Mrs Goelet and Robert, Lady Anne and Lady Isobel and Mr and Mrs Cornelius Vanderbilt.

When the train arrived at Wickford, they were met by the

Steamship, *General,* which was on standby to make the crossing to Newport exclusively for them. When they docked, there was a carriage to take them straight to Ochre Court, where they arrived at about 11p.m., too exhausted that night to appreciate the exotic flowers bedecking every part of the house to welcome them.

In the urgency to reach their destination, it was discovered, after the ship had left, that they had forgotten to carry with them the large pasteboard box of 160 American Beauty roses, sent from Park Avenue for Ochre Court. The stationmaster, *'being a thrifty soul'*, and concerned that these exquisite flowers, valued at $11 for one bud, were going to die before they could reach their destination, took it upon himself to distribute them to all the sick people around Wickford.

Chapter 11
Honeymoon and Homecoming

After all the excitement, not to mention the terrors, of the past few days, Ochre Court was the ideal sanctuary for the newly-weds. It was the epitome of luxury, having been built '*in the Grand Manner*' as recently as 1888 and designed by Richard Morris Hunt, America's leading architect. Even Duke Boris had been overwhelmed by the opulence, and was quoted as saying '*I have never dreamed of such luxury as I have seen in Newport!*' Ochre Court was the very first, and arguably one of the finest of a group of spectacular residences, built in this exclusive resort which became known as 'Millionaires' Point'.

It was built out of creamy limestone, set on the red sandstone cliffs and was designed to replicate a late medieval French Chateau reminiscent of the transitional period of Francis I (1494 - 1547), in which '*high roofs, turrets, whimsical gargoyles and tall chimneys*' were replaced by the more Gothic features of pointed arches and heavy stained glass windows, and so the archways were more rounded and displayed delicate almost lacy ornamentation. It looked exactly like an early Renaissance castle, except that there was no moat.

Inside, the most dominant feature was the Great Hall, which soared to the height of three floors and offered a breathtakingly magnificent view of the Atlantic Ocean.

In fact, poised as it was over the sloping lawns which led directly to the cliffs, one almost had the impression of being on board a boat about to launch out into the waves. This illusion was continued throughout all the impressive reception rooms on the ground floor as they radiated from the hall, each in turn overlooking the sea through long windows, several of which opened as doors onto the terraces.

The private family suites were on the floor above, and each designed to luxuriate in the magnificent ocean vista. The walls were mirror-clad, reflecting both the light and the sea, and were etched with decorative and symbolic motifs of aquatic themes, which were repeated delicately throughout the rooms.

Ochre Court was most certainly constructed as a visible celebration of the Goelet's New World wealth and status, but it was also the dream house of the late Ogden, whose love of the sea had led him to become one of the world's greatest yachtsmen. In this house, the sea was always present within as well as without in the breathtaking panorama.

The interior was a mixture of Medieval church and Royal Chateau, particularly obvious in the Great Hall, and the architect sought to celebrate the importance of his patrons as New World promoters of learning and the Arts, just as his European predecessors had done centuries before. Thus, there were both classical and biblical scenes either painted on ceilings or represented in magnificent ancient stained glass windows, which had been carefully transported, usually from Europe, and reconstructed. There were carvings on pillars and statues soaring up to the magnificent ceiling. A multitude of heraldic devices adorned the walls both indoors and out in the grounds. Similar themes were echoed throughout on priceless Medieval tapestries and wall-hangings, the collecting of which was to remain May's passion throughout her life. Naturally, many of the antiques were imported directly from Europe but where this was not feasible, materials from the Old World were imported, either to be worked on in Rhode Island or else European craftsmen were commissioned to produce the works, which were then transported to America so that maximum authenticity was achieved in their replication.

Thus, the stone on which were carved heraldic designs in the Great Hall came from Caen in Normandy, France. The priceless antique furniture and many of the furnishings had been purchased from noble or royal palaces of France, Spain and Italy, which had fallen on hard times, and they helped to generate the atmosphere of a genuine royal palace.

The State Dining Room was lined in richly-carved panels, probably designed, if not executed, in France and brought to Rhode Island. There was also a huge and unique marble-framed fireplace with two hearths – one on each side – which was thought to be the largest fireplace of its type in the world. The wooden, carved panels in the dining room were topped with gold friezes, all of which were certainly made in France and imported. The fireplace in the ballroom was of white Carrara marble from Italy, as were the decorative scrolls carved around the fireplace and echoed on the ceiling and above each window. The paintings, set in wall-panels throughout the room and lit by tear-drop crystal chandeliers, were also from Europe.

Throughout the reception rooms there were paintings and huge carvings, depicting the mythological characters of the legends of Rome and Greece in the style of many European palaces.

In the Great Hall there were even twelve gigantic, carved human creatures, or carytids, apparently supporting the ceiling with its painted scene of the banquet of the gods. In places, these themes were alternated with religious paintings, or stained glass windows, such as the one over the grand staircase, which was medieval German in style and probably taken from a church during the Reformation. The central panel showed God the Father holding the Ten Commandments, and below him the temptations of the devil were depicted over the heads of the tempted, and exhortations against giving in to these temptations were lettered in Middle German script.

Even the formal gardens and walkways were proof of the Goelet's wealth and yearning for the trappings of nobility experienced abroad. Great European Copper Beeches and Far Eastern Kousa Dogwood, with its dense flower heads surrounded by creamy-white bracts, grew among more native species of trees and bushes, and set between them were sculptures from the Old Classical World.

In all it was a fantastic palace, operated by its twenty-seven house servants, eight coachmen and grooms, and twelve gardeners when the family was in residence.

One particular symbol was repeated in ironwork, bronze and stone throughout the house and gardens, and this was the image of the cygnet. For the cygnet was in the Goelet's coat of arms and was chosen because it represented poetry, grace, music and purity. It was emblazoned on the wall bearing the Goelet motto *Ex Candore Decus,* which meant *Beauty from Splendour,* and referred to the cygnet which will develop into a swan.

After the excitement of recent days, this fairy-tale mansion must have seemed a haven of comfort and luxury. May and Kelso spent their days quietly walking or taking rides in one of the four automobiles at their disposal. All the formalities of their real worlds were relinquished and they just delighted in the joy of each other's company, away from all intrusion.

So simple were their pleasures during those days that one of their bodyguards complained at their lack of diversions and commented on the fact that they were '*even seen to wear the same outer clothes on consecutive days.*' He was also slightly bemused that they arrived home on foot one day after their car had developed a puncture. Activities which were to other people normal were to become for May and Kelso the heart of their relationship. May revelled during these days in the chance to live without the world observing and passing judgement, and she learned that Kelso's love of privacy was to open for her a whole new way of life.

Even when the family party of both their mothers, Robert, Isobel and the Vanderbilts joined them later that week, they managed to maintain a close, relaxed atmosphere, possible principally because it was off season for Millionaires' Point. Fortunately most, if not all, of the other mansions were closed up for the winter, and therefore there was no-one to expect to receive or to issue invitations and intrude into their peace.

The newly-weds, nevertheless, took time to do simple things, such as to visit the members of the staff who had worked so hard to make these days so idyllic. They particularly went out of their way to thank Chief Gardener, Sullivan. May always loved flowers and she was aware of the effort that had gone into providing sufficient magnificent floral displays to embellish every corner of Ochre Point throughout those late November Days. So Kelso and she went down to the greenhouses to express their thanks – much to the stunned delight of Mr Sullivan, who couldn't believe it when Kelso, *'a real live duke'*, took his hand and shook it, while expressing his sincere gratitude.

May also asked Sullivan to convey their thanks to his staff for the *'pretty piece of silver'* that they had gifted for the wedding. She asked him to assure them that she would keep the gift-card bearing all of their names. Indeed, she hinted that she may even have it framed to remind her of them all and their kindness when she was far away in Scotland.

All too soon, their three weeks were over. By then, Lady Anne and Isobel had already long returned to Scotland, to set in motion all the preparations for the bridal couple's homecoming for a family Christmas in Dunbar at Broxmouth House.

But, for Kelso and May, the honeymoon was not yet over, because they planned to travel from New York to France so that they could spend a short period alone together in Paris, before being joined there by Mrs Goelet for a couple of days before making the final stages of their journey to May's new home.

After the fiasco of the wedding, all travel arrangements were kept as secret as possible, but, nevertheless, a rumour did circulate that they were due to travel on the *Kaiser Wilhelm II*.

At the appointed time, a great crowd of reporters and sightseers turned up at the dock, hoping to glimpse the newly-weds. But they were disappointed, and the ship set sail without anyone catching sight of either of them. Even the passenger list displayed on board did not include their names, so those who had come on board, under the pretence of visitors bidding relatives goodbye but hoping rather to get a story – or even, perhaps, photographs – were disappointed and had to leave in haste as the gangplanks were drawn in.

They, and the disappointed onlookers, gradually gave up and left. But the duke and his bride were, in fact, already on board. May and Kelso had arrived incognito, very early, and had been spirited directly to their stateroom by stewards sworn to secrecy.

As it was the finest and most luxurious suite on the boat, which had its own dining room, a delightful, private sitting room, a commodious bedroom with its own bathroom. The Roxburges did not need to leave it to go up on deck, or mix with others, unless they chose to do so. Hence very few of the crew and none of the passengers realized that the couple were actually sailing with them and, moreover, were already safely and most comfortably settled on board. Thus, when the ship sailed, not one journalist had the scoop he had hoped for and it was assumed that the tip-off they had received had been in error.

But, on the second day at sea, to everyone's surprise, a new passenger list was posted, and there, in a column of their own, were the names of the Duke and Duchess of Roxburghe. The subsequent flurry of excitement and curious anticipation was short-lived, however, as the young couple kept very much to themselves and barely ever came on deck throughout the whole voyage. The fact that they were crossing the Atlantic in late November hardly tempted them to seek outdoor pursuits at the expense of their privacy.

After their visit to Paris, the newly-weds finally began their journey home to Britain, where they went directly to London to catch the train north. The decision to spend Christmas at Broxmouth House, Kelso's birthplace, which was now his mother's Dower House, had a two-fold benefit. There, May would have the chance to meet the rest of her new family but also have time to acclimatize herself to Scotland before taking up her position and responsibilities as Mistress of Floors Castle.

The London train brought them to Berwick-upon-Tweed station, the last stop in England before crossing the Scottish border. There, the duke and duchess transferred to a 'special' train, which had been laid on to take them up the east coast, into Scotland and to the town of Dunbar.

If May was apprehensive of meeting the Scottish public after the New York crowds, she was to be very pleasantly surprised.

The townsfolk of Dunbar were genuinely delighted that the young duke had chosen to introduce his bride to Scotland in *their* town – the town of his birth, twenty-seven years earlier – and they turned out in their numbers to give them a '*right hearty welcome*'. But, in Britain, there was an accepted protocol in these matters in the early years of the twentieth century, and it was a matter of civic pride that everyone was determined that it should be observed.

Therefore, although the general public gathered to welcome the bridal couple, the actual station and platform were declared closed to all but the official welcoming party.

Everyone else was allowed to gather outside the railings to watch and to cheer loyally when required.

On this bleak December day, the station buildings and the railings had been decked out in fairy lights, and a cheery red carpet had been laid out on the platform in honour of the occasion.

The train was expected to arrive at 5.55pm, so, at 5.30 the Provost and the entire Town Council met in full civic regalia at the Municipal Buildings in the town square, from where they formed a procession which was led by the North Berwick Pipe Band, the plaid of their Highland uniform providing yet more colour in the bleak winter gloom.

On arrival, the dignitaries arranged themselves into a formal welcoming committee, while the band marched into position to pipe the train into the station.

As the train steamed to a standstill, the stationmaster stepped forward to open the door, Kelso jumped onto the platform and turned to offer his wife his hand. May, well wrapped up from the winter cold but wreathed in smiles, placed her small hand in his as she stepped onto the red carpet and so onto Scottish ground. Kelso bowed in acknowledgement to the men of Dunbar and to the pipers as their music stopped. May waved to the crowd who responded with delight.

Provost Gibb overcame his awe of the situation and stepped forward to greet them, saying the piece he had taken such pains to prepare:

'Your Graces, in the name of the Magistrates, the Town Council, and the inhabitants of Dunbar, I extend to you a right hearty welcome to our royal and ancient burgh. We are

delighted to know that the occasion of her Grace's first visit to Scotland [as duchess] is to Broxmouth Park, the seat of Your Grace's birthplace. During your sojourn there I have no doubt you will enjoy the bright, bracing and invigorating breezes for which our burgh is known. I will not delay Your Graces further as you have had a long train journey, but shall conclude wishing you long life, health and happiness'.

At this, everyone, from the eager crowds who were straining to catch sight of the couple and the guests of honour on the platform, burst into ecstatic cheering and applause which only stopped when Kelso held up his hand to speak. Genuinely touched by the sincerity of their welcome, the duke thanked them briefly on his own behalf and that of his wife. There was another outburst of delighted applause.

After this, the pipers re-formed to pipe the couple to the waiting carriage. Following local custom, there were no horses in the shafts at this point, but a team of '*stalwart coastguardsmen*' were waiting to pull the carriage manually from the station, through the streets to the town boundary where a team of horses had been tethered by the coachmen to wait for them.

The Town Council formed a procession behind the band, and an escort of police fell into step alongside. Meanwhile, two lines of torchbearers appeared to form walking illuminations along each side of the coach.

The moment they had left the station, a brilliant display of rockets and fireworks were set off from the Yeomanry Memorial Stone in the town, and the response of genuinely surprised delight from the young Roxburghes set the crowd off into further cheers and applause.

Amid this spontaneous explosion of good will, the horses were finally hitched in place and the happy couple were merrily sent on their way to Broxmouth Park to enjoy a peaceful Christmas with Kelso's family.

Chapter 12
Homecoming to Kelso

After spending a totally private family Christmas in Dunbar, word was sent to Floors Castle and Kelso town confirming that May was to arrive, finally, at her new home on Tuesday, January 5th 1904, a date that had been suggested a fortnight beforehand. Needless to say, the dignitaries and people of Kelso were already well prepared to give Her Grace a welcome she would never forget.

Their delight was sincerely felt because the people, so many of whom depended on the castle for a living, had been saddened when Lady Anne had vacated Floors Castle to make Broxmouth House her permanent dower home. Obviously the other members of the family who were not yet married had joined their mother.

Now, the imminent return of the duke with a new and beautiful wife was, in every way, a fresh beginning for the estate and the whole town, so the celebrations came from their hearts.

It was a *dreich*, – dreek – dismal, foggy day when they arrived at the station, but the decorations from train to castle were colourful and exuberant. The station itself had been delightfully decorated under the direction of the then station agent, Mr Winton. A special exit had been created by using coloured cloths for screening, and an awning had been erected from where the train would stop to where they would meet their carriage. Underfoot there was a crimson carpet. Everywhere there was a profusion of palms, evergreens, flowers and other pot plants, and many, many flags. As the train steamed up to the platform, the fog-signals were sounded and the crowd, massed outside, cheered.

As in Dunbar, his Grace alighted and handed May down, at which point his chamberlain, Mr Brunton, stepped forward to welcome them and offer his congratulations. They thanked him and shook hands warmly. The other members of the reception committee, from the estate office, the tenantry and from the town added their welcomes and, after each was introduced and thanked, May and Kelso made their way into the waiting open carriage with Mr Brunton to head for Kelso.

May looked radiant, dressed in a costume of wine-coloured cloth, opened at the neck to show cream lace. Her hat was pale heliotrope trimmed with pale purple and white lilac. She wore a sable stole and carried a huge bunch of carnations – her favourite flower, and one that was to be very significant to her in the future, when she was to help to breed new strains of the plant at the Floors Greenhouses.

The waiting crowds were enchanted by her beauty and her charm, and their cheers grew more and more enthusiastic the more she smiled and waved at them. But, despite the lightweight barricades, there was not a single untoward incident.

The Kelso Chronicle described her impact thus: '*the townspeople were quite captivated with the duchess whose comely presence, smiling face and gentle demeanour impressed them most favourably*'.

All the way, the route was lined with cheering people. The cottages and shops in Maxwellheugh, through which they drove, were decked in evergreens and bunting, which certainly added colour to the grey weather and the inhabitants cheered, waving their hats or handkerchiefs.

Had it not been so foggy, May could have glimpsed her new home as they passed along this route, but it was not to be. As they approached Kelso town, they drove across the bridge which was lined with well-wishers, then passed under a floral archway in front of the Roxburghshire Coachworks executed in green and gold, the Roxburghe colours, as it bore a dark green banner on which it said in gold lettering: 'Welcome Home'.

All along the pavements, the cheering crowds thronged and it seemed that every window had someone leaning out, waving to show their pleasure when the duke or duchess acknowledged their greetings.

When they reached the Market Place there was a huge triple, floral archway, curving over the road and on each side over the pavement. On one side hung a banner saying *'Welcome Home'*, and on the other, *'Health and Happiness'*. Having passed through this, the carriage drew up at a specially erected platform, on which the Reception Committee, a large group of prominent local men, had already taken up their positions, having received a phone call from the station to alert them of the ducal approach. Leading them were Provost Crichton Smith, Bailie Ritchie and Bailie Neil, whom Mr Brunton introduced to the Duke and Duchess, who shook them by the hand.

After this, Provost Smith made his address:

'On behalf of the several gentlemen on the platform and the members of the committee charged with the reception arrangements, may it please your Graces, I desire to be permitted, on behalf of the town, to offer you our hearty congratulations on your marriage, and to express our heartfelt wish for your happiness, [Cheers]. Such an event, of course, is of supreme importance in your own lives and in the history of the Roxburghe family, and it is, at the same time, an occasion of no ordinary importance to the inhabitants of this town – [Hear - hear!] - whose pride it has been to know that the relations existing between your Grace's family and themselves have always been of the most cordial nature. [Hear – hear!] and we feel confident that we can rely, in your Grace's case, upon the continuance of these happy relations. [Cheers] We desire most heartily to welcome you both and more especially I may be permitted to extend to your Grace, the duchess, a very special welcome on this, the occasion of your first visit to your new home. [Loud applause.] We feel sure that Floors will have its attractions for you, and we hope that we may frequently have the privilege, as it certainly will be our great pleasure, to see you both in our midst, when you will always have a most cordial welcome. [Hear hear – loud cheers].' The Kelso Mail. Wednesday Jan 6th. At this, Kelso stood up in the carriage to reply and the cheering was ecstatic. Once he could be heard he said:

'Provost Smith, Town Councillors, ladies and gentlemen, it is no easy task for me to reply to the able speech in which your Provost has welcomed us in the name of the town of Kelso. The interests of my family are so much interwoven with those of the town and district of Kelso that it would indeed be

a calamity if good feeling and friendship did not exist between them. [Hear, hear – cheers]. It will be the aim and object of the duchess and myself to foster the continuance of the happy state of affairs which has hitherto made my family so popular among you. [Renewed cheers, and hear, hear]. It is no small compliment to me and it is a great honour to the duchess that she should have today been welcomed in so cordial a manner, coming as she does a stranger in a strange land, [Calls of 'Cheers for the duchess', to which an enthusiastic response was given]. However, I am convinced that the old family saying has again in her case come true – namely that 'no Duke of Roxburghe ever married an ill wife'.

He then mentioned by name a prominent member of the community who was seriously ill, sending him their best wishes, after which he concluded:

'Provost Smith, I must now ask you to accept from the duchess and myself, on behalf of the town of Kelso, our grateful and sincere thanks, for this cordial and warm welcome we have received. [Loud and continuous cheering].' Kelso Mail

Then, the officials made way for Bailie Neil's little granddaughter to approach the duchess, and someone lifted her up to the carriage so that she could offer May a '*very beautiful shower bouquet composed of pink American winter-flowering carnations and lilies of the valley, relieved with asparagus fern and bound with broad white satin ribbon, on either end of which were finely executed hand-painted designs of the British and American flags*'. Kelso Mail.

May delightedly expressed her thanks and the procession prepared to move on. Every building in town was dressed in bunting, greenery and many British and American flags and, as it was such a dark day, lights were lit in every window, and left burning throughout the evening when the revelries continued, the gentlemen of the Reception Committee attending a cake and wine banquet in the Billiard Room at the Cross Keys Hotel in the centre of town.

But May and Kelso continued on the final stage of their journey to Floors.

As they drove over the cobbled road to the entrance lodge, the coachmen drew the horses to a standstill. A group of estate workmen moved forwards to unhitch the horses from their shafts, and, as in Dunbar, they themselves stepped into their places and began to draw the carriage up the driveway.

As they were about to set off, the lodge-keeper's little girl, Jeannie Peattie, shyly came forward and presented May with another 'shower bouquet', this time of roses and lilies of the valley, saying as she did so: *'From Mr and Mrs Peattie's children with best wishes for health and happiness'*.

And so May came to Floors.

*****

Floors Castle is an exotic and magical castle, which had evolved from a fairly plain, simple tower house, built on a rolling natural terrace sweeping down to the River Tweed and overlooking an undisturbed view of the Cheviot Hills. It lies opposite the site of Roxburghe Castle, one of the earliest and reputedly the strongest of the Scottish border castles, which had been built along the former march with England, to rebuff invaders. But Floors Castle was never designed to be a fortress.

On the contrary, in 1721, the 1st duke commissioned the fabled William Adam to expand an existing residence into an elegant, symmetrical Georgian country house, the epitome of secured opulence.

Just over a century later, the 6th duke employed William Playfair, an eminent architect from Edinburgh to remodel the castle. Drawing inspiration from the ornamental, style of Herriot, his predecessor, Playfair moved away from the classical to the romantic and ornamental to create a palace that would be fantastic but welcoming. Even in the winter gloom when May arrived that January, she would have seen as she was swept between the identical outstretched arms of the warm sand-stone building to the portico the riot of mini turrets and cupolas that decorated this huge but elegant edifice.

It was everything – and more – that Ochre Court had aspired to be. It was, in truth, a castle with an ancient pedigree that had grown and expanded over the centuries to accommodate the wealth and status of its incumbents. Each feature of its internal décor displayed the best in design of its period and exulted in the rich imported or local materials of which it was built.

The windows throughout bore no resemblance to the narrow slitted apertures of military castles, but had all the airiness of Georgian casements and looked out in all directions over rolling parkland and manicured gardens.

When she awoke the following morning and gazed out either over the tree-lined driveway she had been unable to see on the previous evening, flanked by wooded areas and paddocks, or over the over-sweep of gardens running down to the racing river Tweed and the breathtaking views beyond, reaching to the skyline of the rugged Cheviot hills, May must have felt the surge of dawning love for this, her beautiful new home.

Chapter 13
Settled At Last

May's devotion to Floors was to manifest itself over the years in the way she used her creativity to put her own influence on the décor, and yet to maintain the integrity of the castle's design.

She brought with her the beginnings of a priceless collection of 17th century Flemish tapestries; inherited others when her mother died, and over the years she and Kelso kept a keen watch on salesrooms in Britain and Europe for others of equal merit coming on to the market.

Some of the earliest ones were so huge that windows were filled in in the ballroom to create adequate hanging space to display such valuable works of art to their best advantage.

Aware of the value of the traditional paintings which adorned almost every wall throughout the castle, May began a new collection of celebrated paintings in the modern style which she displayed with taste, bringing the twentieth century into Floors with subtle skill.

In a room she had decorated in the style of a room in Versailles, and furnished in a gilt suite in the style of Louis XVI that she had brought to Floors, she displayed paintings by Henri Matisse, Pierre Bonnard, Augustus John and Sir Matthew Smith.

Her passion for flowers and all growing things found expression, not only in the experiments with developing new strains of carnations but also in the lay-out design of areas of the garden close to the house, some of which are still evident today. She worked with the head gardener to develop the walled garden into a productive fruit garden with espaliered apple trees and soft fruit trees, all of which enriched the excellent cuisine served from the castle kitchens. In addition, the extensive greenhouses provided the more exotic fruits.

Floors Castle and their London home were always filled with flowers. This was to continue long after Kelso died in 1932, evident from the carefully kept florists' receipts among her personal effects, showing costs that would have exceeded what her servants would expect to earn for a whole week's work – if not an entire month.

From the start, May slipped easily into the role of wife and duchess, equally at home accompanying Kelso on official duties as she was playing hostess to their many distinguished friends, either at gracious banquets or at shooting party dinners.

She even entertained King George and Queen Mary in the beautiful dining room at Floors, which was resplendent in the famous Roxburghe silver and silver-gilt tableware. She loved hosting or attending card games, which were highly fashionable in Edwardian Society and were to be a lasting interest throughout her life. As a connoisseur collector of tapestries, she developed a genuine talent for tapestry-work in her own right, working with considerable competence and artistry.

But May was also a young lady of the twentieth century

and, to Kelso's delight, she took part in more active entertainments like fishing, where she could compete on an equal footing with any of their gentlemen guests whatever the weather conditions.

Kelso also respected May's judgement over the choice of artefacts or major purchases for their home, which was very unusual for the time regardless of the fact that her fortune contributed massively to their expenditure.

The duke was to find the 'obligatory' round of social engagements more palatable with May at his side, although to the end he always preferred those which encompassed sporting activities. Hence, although they frequently joined King Edward at house parties, Kelso preferred it when they were included in the royal party at Ascot or the Derby with Edward and, after his death, with King George V.

Kelso's friendship with the king continued and flourished and, as his wife, May was courteously welcomed into this inner circle.

Nevertheless, it took her many years to really feel fully accepted in her own right, and this was revealed in a touching note that she pencilled onto the envelope of a letter she had received from Queen Mary. For many years, May had annually sent a generous gift for the queen's chosen charity, and each year there would be a kindly but formal note of thanks from the queen, usually accompanied by a signed, unpublished photograph of the Royal Family, all of which she kept and treasured in a little leather wallet.

Then, one year, May was both surprised and delighted when the queen made it a little more personal by addressing her informally.

May wrote on the envelope: "*She called me May!*"

The feisty character that had asserted May's independence throughout the years of being pursued for hand and fortune was never to leave May, and she didn't tolerate fools gladly. The experience of Press behaviour at her wedding meant that she never pandered to members of the Press. This attitude was endorsed by Kelso, who always maintained his sense of personal privacy which, obviously, now extended to his family.

Hence, after the 'honeymoon' period of curiosity and intrigue was over about this new, beautiful, and fantastically wealthy lady in their midst, there was a cooling off period from the press who contented themselves with reporting routine functions straightforwardly and without undue comment or elaboration.

Besides, at that period there was still an unwritten code which was almost always respected by the British Press, which was that courtesy must be observed towards all members of aristocracy and their families. But the American Press and some of the burgeoning magazines in Britain resented the lack of information forthcoming from May Roxburghe, and they resorted to a veiled hostility, choosing the one area of her life in which May was most vulnerable. That was the fact that there was still no sign of an heir, even several years into the marriage.

There was much cruel speculation on what could happen to May's inheritance should she die without issue, because Kelso had reacted so strongly against having one of the demeaning financial contracts that characterized most of the Trans-Atlantic alliances. By so doing, it was surmised that he may have failed to insure against the possibility of failing to produce an heir.

Much as this must have hurt the couple, they maintained a dignified silence, while May consulted doctors both in Britain and on the Continent, in the hope that she may one day have a child.

May underwent many examinations and experimental treatments in the hope that she would conceive. At one point, she spent considerable time in Germany under the care of a Swiss gynaecologist. At that time it was not considered seemly to include the husband in such procedures, and the almost daily, touching letters from Kelso reveal how hard this ordeal was for him, too; but the couple maintained a level of privacy, which managed to avoid too much comment in the Press.

Kelso visibly continued with his duties on the estate and in London where he attended a sufficient number of functions to deflect curiosity.

May, meanwhile, was seen to meet up with her mother in Paris and travel with her, so the real purpose of the visit was concealed. Kelso periodically joined them for a couple of days and then returned to Britain.

Nevertheless, there was sporadic press speculation and, although the reporters capitalized on *their* perception of the situation, ordinary folk were far more sympathetic towards May and sent her letters offering all sorts of quaint advice to improve her chances of becoming pregnant.

As so often happens, however, in such cases, once the Roxburghes seemed to accept the situation as it stood and returned to their ordinary lives, May suddenly discovered she was, at long last, pregnant after ten years of marriage.

The announcement was received with a genuine spirit of congratulation, if not delight, by most of the press, but one particularly vitriolic magazine made the announcement on a black-edged, full page spread in the guise of a sympathy message to May's American sister-in-law, Anne Breese, wife of Alastair, consoling her that *her* eldest son was no longer destined to be the 9th Duke.

But nothing could dampen the couple's joy when, finally, their only child, George Innes-Ker, Lord Bowmont – who was throughout life to be called 'Bobo', was born safe and well in Chesterfield House, their London home, on 7th September 1913.

Every newspaper carried a rapturous report of the little boy's birth, and His Majesty, King George, was immensely pleased for them, and immediately sent his warmest congratulations together with the proposal that he and the queen should, themselves, be the child's godparents.[2]

The joy of the little family was to be short-lived, however, for just after Bobo's first birthday the Great War broke out, and Kelso immediately rejoined his Regiment and was sent to the Front.

In the event, his war service was to be short but dramatic, and there is a graphic account of what happened in the letters he wrote home to May.

The Regiment was dispatched to Belgium and landed with some disarray in ZeeBrugge. Kelso, as an experienced soldier, was appalled at the haphazardness and incompetence of the whole operation:-

---

[2] A copy of the king's letter is included at the end of this book.

Sat 10th Oct. 2.30pm Beernem
My Darling,

I suppose the censor will mutilate this but I write freely as you are not likely to divulge any news – well it seems an age since we left and we have had some bad days which do no credit to the powers that be and the military organization is indeed a marvel!

Our sea journey was curious, the regiments were split up anyhow – on our boat 2 squadrons Blues and 1st 2nd Lifeguards Harold in command and no vet or officer or doctor. We landed at ZeeBrugge between Ostend and Antwerp and had various orders and counter orders and at last, when it was dark ended up by bivouacking on the sea shore, a new sort of strategic post for cavalry with the sea at our backs and canals and barbed wire in front. I can only liken our night to that one might spend in a golf bunker – it was devilish cold and rifles and everything got filled with sand. The next day we eventually moved to Bruges, a jolly old town, the flowers and trees, interesting, and ended up spending the night in a large building evidently used for storing large quantities of Bay trees with which it was surrounded and slept soundly only waking occasionally when the horses kicked near our feet - Yesterday we witnessed the retreat of the Belgian army from Antwerp – they are a motley collection and don't look like fighting and they say they are done to a turn and are to be passed to the rear to gain heart and refit. Their equipment and guns look antiquated and one marvels they could put up any show against the Germans.

Our horses are well since they have not been given a chance since we left on 5th and a day to let them pick up is all that is wanted. We hear little or no news but hope all goes well

– I'm scribbling this during a long wait of which we have many, but will write again soon.

Love and kisses to my baby,
Your own,
Boysie

The next letter May was to receive was more upbeat and full of news.

14th October, 9.30 a.m.
No 2 Nr French Frontier

'My Darling
    I've had no time to write since my last for we have been continuously on the move not really doing any good and wearing out the horses - Today we have not moved off yet though we are prepared to turn out at any minute. Our Brigade Staff have shown no consideration for the horses and their incompetence of which there was ample evidence before we left England has been more than maintained - for instance - the men drew no rations for two and a half days then were given three days late at night - the bulk having to be wasted - our billets and bivouacs have been badly chosen and they seem to forget that horses need watering and feeding when out from 6 a.m. to 8 and ten at night- My own horses have held out well except the chestnut which had bad food but now is better - but my ass of a groom has given it a very bad sore back which will take weeks to get right. We are all well and hearty and are now joined up to French's army and yesterday Alastair, Sars[?] Lottie and all the other cavalry are nearby. Yesterday while we were making a flank march to join up I went off down a side road to guard against attack. I luckily was on the lookout with two sentries and about 8 men ready when I spied a [?] patrol of 12 trotting down the road towards us (the natives having warned me there was one about) we opened fire and killed one, shot through the head, wounded another

who got away with the rest who bolted, and got one of their horses which however, had to be shot afterwards as it was so done up. This was the first man the Regiment or Brigade had accounted for so that my mob were very elated. We hear no news of how things are going and though as I write our guns are in action about two miles off we don't know what is going on. I have slept every night, except one in an open shed and last night in a long cart beside Charlie Ken, luckily we have not had much rain but heavy hoar frost one night, when my pillow was in consequence quite white and wet but I got it dried in a cottage the following evening. The Belgians are wonderful to men and officers, dash out at all villages with bread, coffee, apples etc. and assist to water the horses. The country we have been working in up to date is very enclosed and intensely cultivated and I don't know why more natives don't get killed as they are always hanging about. I am well equipped but have too much kit which is a fault on the right side. When you send any foods essence of cocoa with (sasim ??) is what I find most useful but the tins of the former should be small, slabs of chocolate (munched with ration biscuits) are also very useful, we buy eggs occasionally and get bully beef and other farm rations the same as issued to the men - but when we get further on I don't suppose we shall find much in the country. I saw Bendor in a motor yesterday and Hugo Baring with 10th Hussars but had no time to talk with either. We had a great laugh the other night as Alastair's former servant fell into the farm cesspool at our bivouac. We have reveille daily at 4am quite dark and ready to move at 6am so that by night we are ready to lie down. Your letter of 7th has just arrived and by it I suppose you will now be at Floors. I think continually of you and the infant and of the fun we will have when I get back. I have no doubt that the Colonel's letters give fairly full details of our movements so keep in touch with Sarah. I'll write again as soon as I can, in the meantime cheer up, I'm well and hearty but only wish we knew we were to have an off day today. Much love to my mother and tell your mother all about me.

Your loving,
Boysie'

By the 19th October, the war was over for Kelso as he was wounded. He managed to scribble a pencil message to May on a scrap of paper which was delivered, folded in to the General Surgeon's report from the field station, dated 19th October.

'My darling,

I've just got into a field dressing station having got knocked over this morning - it's not a bad wound - grazed my left testicle and went through my left thigh, missing the artery - I had to be left in a cottage for an hour as we had to retire but they came back and fetched me as the Germans also retired. It's not bad and the bone is not touched so don't worry and I shall soon be home again.

Tell my mother not to fuss as I'm all right and cheer up yourself. The attack was on Roulers -

Yesterday I did well killing a German with my sword. Much love,

Your own
Boysie. <u>Cheer up</u>.'

The Surgeon's letter was marked "On Active Service" and stamped "Passed by Censor No: 1028"

'Dear Duchess,

I promised to send the enclosed on. Don't worry as he is wonderfully well considering.

He is full of cheer & his wound is quite clean and should heal rapidly. I was present when he was brought into the dressing station. I am awfully glad he was so lucky to get off as light - It has been a tough scrap & of course the 7th Brigade all did well. We have suffered sad to say rather severely.

Yours truly
Ph(?) Lammis
G.S. 111 Cav. Div.'

Also dated the 19th October was this brief note from Kelso, who had obviously been transported back to the UK:

'We weren't told where we were to be taken till we got to Waterloo at 2p.m. Thursday.'

But he was taken to one of the emergency hospitals for which his own Chesterfield House had been commissioned and from where he wrote this letter to May:

'My Darling,

I've tried to wire on every occasion to you since I was wounded last Monday to tell you I was all right - but of course nothing ever was sent - and probably the first news you got was my wire from Southampton.

Well, I got knocked over last Monday near Roulere, the rifle bullet grazing my left testicle and going through my left thigh, high up, luckily missing bones and arteries. The wounds are all clean and doing well so don't fuss for I feel well and hearty.

I have little feeling in my left foot at present as some nerves are probably severed but they say that will soon be all right. I was so lucky as we had to retire soon after I was hit and I was carried 50yards and left in a farm house. The Germans advanced to within 300yards and then retired and after about 2 hours three of my own men came round and wheeled me away in a barrow - I've travelled with others with various delays and halts practically since then, the only uncomfortable parts being 6 hours in motor ambulance over awful roads and the French railway train.

Look in on your way from the station and you'll be surprised how well I am.

Much love, your own, Boysie.'

Just before Christmas that year, he was joined by both of his brothers, each of whom had, by then, been wounded. Alastair, an officer in the Blues like Kelso, had received a shot in the head but was to make a full recovery and, eventually, was to become one of the founder members of the Royal Flying Corps.

Robin, their younger brother, was in the Irish Guards and he had been blown up and left for dead on the battlefield. He came round to find himself a prisoner of war, but he escaped when the Germans were pushed back in the Battle of the Marne, after which he too was invalided home to Chesterfield

House[3]. He was later to recover fully and become a military attaché in Paris.

Kelso, however, was to walk with a limp for the rest of his life and always needed a walking cane.

After the war, life continued much as before for Kelso and May.

Although May was fiercely proud of Bobo, she did not particularly adapt to motherhood. She left control of the nursery in the hands of a formidable nanny called Saward – pronounced Sword, who was quite capable of sending a letter with a barely veiled criticism of her mistress if she considered her to be spending too much time in London, – albeit being involved in war work or visiting her husband – at the expense of her son. In one such note, she stated that the duchess *may* have seen the little boy's first steps had she been home in Floors, not to mention the appearance of his early teeth.

Whether May rebuked such insubordination is not possible to ascertain, but there was certainly no dismissal. Indeed, May must have considered her to be indispensable as a nanny, because she was still very much in evidence – and control – when Bobo's cousin, Arthur Collins, son of Lady Evelyn, came from Eton with Bobo to spend holidays at Floors.

Even as an octogenarian Knight of the Realm, Sir Arthur still recalled with some trepidation how his cousin and he took pains to avoid both Nanny Saward and 'Aunt May' during those holidays for fear of recrimination - to the point where

---

[3] Chesterfield House was their own London home, used as a hospital for officers.

they preferred to climb out of the billiard room window and escape to hide in the woods.

Thus life continued for the 8th duke and his duchess, and in November, 1928, they celebrated their silver wedding anniversary. May's gift to Kelso was the installation of the imposing and beautiful entrance gates that are still in evidence today.

In a letter to his sister, Evelyn, thanking her for an anniversary gift, Kelso reflects that despite whatever problems they had shared, the marriage had been a good one. But it was not destined to last, for barely four years later, in 1932, when May and he attended a funeral at Wilton, home of the Pembrokes, Kelso collapsed with a heart attack and died. Bobo was 19.

May, herself, was to live only another five years, during which time she kept firm control of Bobo's expenditure, even though he was by now an officer in the Blues and a duke.

She gradually cut herself off from most of the rest of the family during these years, and was remembered as a tiny figure sitting at her tapestry loom alone in the huge ballroom at Floors.

Spurred on perhaps by a need for independence, Bobo married when he was only 24, and May moved permanently into their post-war London house at Carlton House Terrace, surrounding herself with flowers and only venturing forth to play cards or to gamble in Crockfords.

It was in London that she finally died in 1937.

Post Script Letters from a Duke

Whenever Kelso was apart from May, he wrote to her almost daily and his letters are a mixture of love, loneliness and every day chat about how he was passing the time without her.

Several of the examples printed below show how difficult he found the periods of separation when May was in France or Germany, consulting specialists about her apparent infertility.

Whilst accepting the conventions that excluded him from his wife's side at such a time, he nevertheless wanted to show her support while she was 'getting on with her job'.

He was grateful that Mrs Goelet was with May, but on a couple of occasions used that as an excuse to cross the Channel apparently to thank his mother-in-law and visit her before she left on other travels but in reality to rejoin his wife for a short period.

Sadly, we do not have the letters and wires that May sent to Kelso, but we know from what he says that he looked forward immensely to receiving them and they gave him some comfort.

Spring 1904 from Floors to the Duchess of Roxburghe, Claridges Hotel, Brook Street.

'My Darling,

I am low as I have yet no letter from you but I fear you were tired after your long journey. As to our sport, there was a hard white frost last night which was not very good for rabbits. However, we got 350.

Bertie Hyde did not but went fishing to Upper Water, getting one of 21lbs in the 'Slater' (?) and as the wind got up he moved down after lunch to lower Water and got 3 -21; 15; 14 – not a bad day but there are not many fish.

It looks like a wild, windy day tomorrow so we may have some sport. Duffy arrived last night about 11.30 quite pleased with himself.

I do hope you are getting on with your job and are comfortable and are amusing yourself – do write me your news as I does ye miss and... about in that big bed.

Goodbye my darling and God bless you. I will write again tomorrow evening.

From your own
Bumble

May 8th 1905
to The Duchess of Roxburghe, Hotel Ritz Place Vendome, Paris.
From 7 Carlton Gardens, Pall Mall

My Darling,

A thousand thanks for your wire which cheered me up a bit on getting back from polo after a heavy defeat – but I think I played well though I got v. tired not being fit and my ponies played well considering it was their first game. The house is v. nice & everyone is settling down & as yet no complaints. There is a safe the key of which Lady Dudley had left in a letter for you, also ample flower vases I discovered in the basement and I don't see there's much (problem) when we get a few flowers up etc.

Sutherland tells an awful tale – poor Sandy escaped when we left for the station & was found in close company with his own dog – an Aberdeen – v. stupid of them to lose her & v. vulgar of her. However the vet to whom she was taken is not certain that she has been attacked and has injected something to try & stop it if it did so that she may not breed mongrels.

I lunched in Barracks & found many friends – tonight I dine with A. Brassey, Buck Barclay & Henry Meade at Carlton & will write you our doings tomorrow.

Goodbye, my darling. Bless you & think of your own
Bumble

My Darling,

I was so low leaving and feel lonely and lost & had a deadly dull journey – but it won't be for long & you must come back on Thursday.

Don't let them do what they did for me and reserve your compartment in the 2nd part of the train for I had to change into the 1st to get some food & had one seat in the corner of a carriage in which were two dressmakers, one a cross between Mrs Moore and the Duchess of Devonshire - & most of the spare room in the carriage filled with flowers.

The servants are up all night & the house fairly straight considering they only arrived this morning but they seem satisfied which is the great thing. I am to see footmen on Monday or Tuesday so please think of me with pity.

The crossing was v. bad. I sat on the upper deck all the way but got a bit wet all the same. A lot of people travelling ... a good many soldiers home from India.

I hear that Sarah's little boy died tonight. V.sad if it is true, as it must be, but I will write you definitely tomorrow.

Goodbye my Darling I am going back weary to my lonely bed,

your own
Bumble

June '06 to May in Hotel d'Angleterre, Germay – now Kelso signs with a new nickname – 'Boysie'

I dined last night with Lady H--- & sat between her and Lady E. Shaw. Not v. exciting meal and torrential rain spoilt the Spencer House Ball when the gardens had been beautifully lit up. I did not go to the ball but trotted back to bed tired and alone. ----

Tonight is Grosvenor House Ball which is sure to be good & I may make my one appearance for the season.

June '07
'My Darling.

I thought you would be amused about Duffy. There is no more to tell except that my mother said she should never entertain it putting it down to the plea of money and that if she had ever had any conception of it she would have taken care they would not have met so often ....

I have outlived my bad cards and have won nicely of late.

Saturday 30th June 06
'My Darling,

I was so excited to get your wire last night and conclude that you are feeling your affairs are coming on and will leave Monday night and arrive Paris and will meet you at the station. I am so looking forward and excited at the idea of being with you again and hope you are not feeling too pulled down. We will make any further plans when we meet.
I conclude that your mother will not have sailed & that we shall find her still in Paris.'

Monday – to May in Germany starts with a report with cuttings of an excellent polo match then continues:-

'anyhow, I shall leave for Paris the day I get your wire. My darling, I have been so lonely and am so looking forward to starting my second honeymoon.

Dick tells me Mrs Astor was at Devonshire House & looked v. well, was not wearing the (?) Diamond but some moderate pearls.'

To May from Chesterfield House
'My Darling,

Your letter enclosing Mrs Astor's amused me v. much. They didn't waste much time did they? And I hope we'll be as successful after your cure.

Wire me directly you think of moving to Paris and I shall dash over as I am sick to death of London. I am glad you refused Londonderry's for it would be a pity to undo the good of your cure by tearing about and it's no great catch...

... Lots of love, my darling – I am longing to be with you again from your own
Boysie'

Monday
'My Darling,

I got back this morning and found 2 nice letters from you awaiting me. Cheer up and it will soon be over.

Well, my party at Reigate was not v. exciting and I missed some pal of my own age. Yesterday after lunch I played golf with Lady C- while most of the party went off in motors after H.M. to see some old garden.

They say his chauffeur drives at a terrific and dangerous pace, along narrow lanes but that H.M. Likes it. Amongst other things they ran over a dog though the King never knew or was told of it.

I came up early this morning & punctured by Wandsworth, so got a tram and and came on to Westminster Bridge and from there by cab. Mrs Ronnie asked me again for next Sunday but I demurred as I didn't know when I would start to meet you – But I don't think I'll go.

Am just back from lunch at my mother's. She says you must not breathe a word about Duffy. She was evidently fair with him & said that he left in tears.

They say that Vanderbilt girl is engaged to Ld Falconer but it's the first I have heard of it. I dine tonight with the Jackdaws, my other gaities this week being dinners at Gavens & Lowerton's but I'm sick of London & long to be with you again.

Goodbye, my Darling – lots of love & kisses
from your own
Boysie

I won a bit off H.M. at bridge playing with Mrs Keppel who was v. stuffy.

Duffy proposed to Evelyn at Earl's Court. When he turned up (at Mother's) I did not, of course, say anything but left hurriedly as I foresee a scene . My Mother being very averse to it & though I am v. fond of Duffy, I don't think it would work, for what could they live on?

Well, as to Byrecleugh, it won't do to ask Duffy now, but, as you have asked Evelyn I will write and ask Guy & we must think of another man or so though in a bad year like this Old Brown & 4 others would do.

I haven't yet gathered any Ascot news though most people must have lost over Pretty Polly.

Floors. 24.06.06
My Darling,

I am writing this before leaving for the 2 o'clock train which will land me in London tonight. I dearly enjoyed my few days here but have been v. lonely but I think it has urged them all on for the wate is sadly behind hand and will take a long time yet to finish. The steps are well in hand as are also the boxes in the back stable yard.

I had a good look round the farm last night. Oliver speaks well of crops etc. and Bennet, who is now in charge of the cow byre, has already tidied things up tremendously. There are a good few rats and (?) and I got a few........

Have told them we shall be back about 10th July. The garden looks well and your herbaceous border should be a success. Street complains of the numbers of stakes it will take and wants espaliers at the back of it.

I hear the 1st Jersey calf we bred here & called 'Crocus' took 1st prize in a strong class in Edinburgh & that the dairymaid took some prizes with butter.

I do so miss you, my Darling, and am longing to have you back. Write me if you approve of my going to Paris 2nd July to say goodbye to your Mother –provided you can get there by the 5th.

Of Harrold, pals are going to give him a gold cigarette box like they gave me & I thought I would fetch up my silver-gilt lighter and have it copied as a gift from us both. What do you think?

Write me how the doctor thinks you are doing.

Newspapers and Periodicals Referenced in this Book

Kelso Chronicle

Kelso Mail

Berwickshire News and Adveriser 1869-1957

Southern Reporter

The Sketch

London Illustrated News

New York Herald

The World

North America Philadelphia

New York American

Floors Castle, Kelso, Roxburghe, seat of the Dukes of Roxburghe.

Henry John Innes-Ker, "Kelso". 8th Duke of Roxburghe.

May Goelet, millionairess bride of the 8th Duke of Roxburghe.

"Kelso" with his son Lord Bowmont or "Bobo".

May Goelet, Duchess of Roxburghe

Henry John Innes-Ker, 8th Duke of Roxburghe

BALMORAL CASTLE.

Sept 11th 1913.

My dear "Bumble"

I must send you a line of most hearty congratulations on the birth of your son & heir & I am so glad to hear both the Duchess & the little boy are doing well. It would give both the Queen & myself much pleasure to become Godparents to your son if you & the

Duchess wished it. I can well understand your joy at becoming a father after waiting so many years.

Hoping the Duchess will make a speedy recovery & with many kind messages to her from the Queen & myself

Believe me
very sincerely yours
George R.I.